The HAPPY LEADER PLAYBOOK

A Science-Backed Guide to Supercharging Energy and Impact

JESSICA LYONFORD

The Happy Leader Playbook Copyright © 2025 by Jessica Lyonford.

Published by Prominence Publishing.

The Happy Leader Playbook/Lyonford, Jessica. -- 1st ed.

ISBN: 978-1-990830-79-2

Dear Happy Leader,

I see you.

I see you choosing people over profit, even when the world tells you efficiency matters more. I see you showing up with courage and compassion—prioritizing mental well-being, building trust and creating a culture where people feel valued as whole, complex humans. I see you challenging the status quo and leading with your gut, your heart and your soul, even when it's hard.

You're not following the old rules—you're rewriting them. And that takes boldness. It takes resilience. It takes energy.

You know, deep down, that happiness isn't a luxury—it's essential. It fuels connection, creativity and success. You see the potential in people and believe that when teams feel energized, engaged and supported, they'll not only hit their goals—they'll surpass them. You're driven by a vision of leadership that lifts others up, that builds communities that thrive and that creates impact far beyond the bottom line.

But let's be honest—this path isn't easy. Leading with intention and purpose in a world that often values hustle over humanity can feel like swimming against the current. It's exhausting. It's lonely. And sometimes, you wonder if it's even worth it.

I'm here to tell you that it is.

Because your energy changes everything.

When you lead with happiness—when you show up with purpose, gratitude and optimism—you create a shift. The energy you bring lifts your team, your family and your community. It changes how people show up at work, how they connect with each other and how they go home at the end of the day. Your leadership reaches farther than you may ever see. And the world needs more of that. The world needs more of *you*.

This book is for you. It's for the leaders brave enough to reimagine what's possible—for themselves, for their teams and for the spaces and places they influence every day. Together we'll explore how to cultivate happiness intentionally—not as a fleeting feeling, but as a skill you can practice.

By the end of this book, you'll know how to design your days to fuel your energy, build teams that thrive and face challenges with clarity and resilience—all while staying true to yourself.

You'll learn how to harness The Eight Pillars of Happiness. You'll discover how intentional Power-Ups can transform your energy and help you create meaningful momentum. And you'll see how, as a Happy Leader, you don't just create results—you create a legacy of belonging and connection.

This is more than leadership—it's a movement.

Let this book be your guide and your support. You're not alone on this journey. There's a growing community of leaders like you—Happy Leaders who are choosing to prioritize happiness not because it's easy, but because it's the way forward.

Thank you for showing up. Thank you for leading with joy and resilience. Thank you for believing that happiness can change the way we work, the way we live and the way we connect with one another.

I see you. I believe in you. And I'm here to walk this path with you.

So let's begin. Let's take this bold, joyful step together. Because you already have everything you need to lead with energy, impact and purpose. The world is ready for you—and you're ready for this.

jessica lyonford

Table of Contents

Introduction

"To me, a leader is someone who holds themselves accountable for finding potential in people and processes. And a joyful leader does it with heart and purpose."

— Brené Brown

This isn't your typical leadership book. Yes, we'll talk about leadership, but from a perspective that sees you as a whole person, not just the role you play at work. Because you and I both know your life outside of work affects everything—your energy, creativity and capacity to lead. And what happens inside those walls? It flows right back into your personal life, impacting how you feel, think and connect with the people and moments that matter most to you.

If you're fighting burnout, struggling with work-life balance or feeling forced to choose between people and profit, this book offers a new path. It's a guide to a different kind of leadership, one rooted in the science of happiness and designed to energize every part of your life. Imagine waking up each day empowered to lead with joy and purpose. And imagine your team operating to its full potential because your leadership is grounded in human flourishing, not just results. That's the impact of happiness as a practice. And that's what we're here to explore together.

I DIDN'T SET OUT TO BECOME A HAPPINESS CONSULTANT.

High school me would've laughed at the idea. Back then, people saw me as smart, creative and a high achiever—traits that didn't prioritize happiness or fulfillment at all. Like many of you, I was driven by the idea that if I just reached certain benchmarks, happiness would naturally follow.

And for a while, I thought I'd made it. I studied advertising and sociology in college, driven by a fascination with people, culture and how human behavior can shift with the right inputs. I launched a successful career in advertising, leading campaigns for global brands and, on paper, living the good life. But in reality, I felt empty. Even as I earned the titles, projects and paychecks I thought would bring me happiness, I was still searching for something meaningful.

If you've ever felt successful on the outside but disconnected on the inside, you know what I mean. I'd reached a point where my actions and my values were deeply misaligned, and my energy and engagement suffered for it. I was using my leadership skills to influence people, but often for outcomes I didn't believe in. And it was exhausting. That sense of disconnection grew until it became burnout, forcing me to pause and reevaluate what had gotten me there—and what needed to change.

DESIGN THINKING TAUGHT ME TO APPROACH HAPPINESS AS SOMETHING WE CAN CREATE.

When I started exploring the then-emerging discipline of design thinking, everything began to click. I realized I could use the same principles of psychology and design that I'd mastered in advertising but for a purpose aligned with my values. I'd spent years learning how to influence decisions, but now I saw those same tools in a new light—as ways to create positive change and design environments where people could engage at their best.

It was then that I understood that happiness could be intentionally designed into our lives and work. Design thinking taught me to build experiences that cultivate genuine fulfillment—where happiness wasn't a side effect but an intentional design element. I learned how every detail, from environment to relationships to goal-setting, can impact energy and shape how we navigate the world. I saw that happiness could be designed for, systematically and with intention.

IMAGINE A WORLD WHERE HAPPINESS IS PART OF THE DESIGN.

As a society, we've already proven we can use psychology to shape our world—though often, we do it in ways that aren't ideal. My advertising career is proof of that. I spent over 15 years crafting messages to spark desire and drive decisions, pushing people to buy things they didn't actually need. And advertising isn't alone in this. Consumer culture, media, politics and workplace management often rely on primal motivators like fear, scarcity and urgency to influence behavior.

Think about how often fear is used as a motivator. Politicians use it to drive votes. Brands use it to drive sales. Social media uses it to drive engagement. Even headlines use fear as the main motivator to drive engagement. "You're Probably Making This Huge Mistake Right Now" and "10 Dangerous Things You Do Every Day Without Realizing It" certainly aren't written to make you feel good.

And while we've designed so much of our world around fear, we've largely left happiness out of the equation. So, what if we used happiness to drive behavior?

Imagine what would happen if we approached happiness with that same level of purpose and intention. Instead of relying on fear or urgency, we could use the science of human flourishing to create environments, routines and relationships that help people feel truly fulfilled. Happiness drives collaboration, creativity, resilience and productivity. And when we design with happiness in mind, we're building a world that helps people not only function but flourish.

And the benefits extend to real workplace challenges, too—think about the impact on retention, on team morale and on adapting to changes like hybrid work. Happiness-focused leadership could address all of these by creating spaces where people feel psychologically safe, where they're inspired to bring their best and where they're supported to grow.

THIS BOOK PROVIDES HAPPY LEADERS A BETTER WAY.

And I'm here to share it with you—to help you design a happier world for yourself and your people–whether that's the team you lead, your family at home or the communities you serve. In these pages, you'll find specific, actionable steps that will take the science of happiness from the abstract to the practical, giving you the power to create more joy and resilience in every aspect of your life and leadership.

We'll start by getting a good understanding of what happiness is and why it matters so much. The first section of the book is the science part. This is where I'm going to share a lot of research about happiness that wasn't available until recently. Because when we know better, we can do better. This will hopefully give you an entirely new perspective on happiness and your relationship with it. We'll spend an entire chapter looking at how energy works before learning The Eight pillars of Happiness and how to use them to create more positive energy—happiness—in your world.

Then, in the second part of the book we'll break down how to lead for impact. This is where we put all that new wisdom around happiness and human flourishing to work for us. We'll learn about Power-Ups and how to use them at home, at work and in our relationships to boost positive energy when and where we need it most. This section covers a lot of ground and provides a ton of real-world strategies, which you can tailor to your life, your team and your specific needs.

And finally, the last section of the book is all about sustaining energy to keep the momentum going. It's about how to live and lead supercharged. It's here where we'll get very specific on how to define happiness and success for yourself so that you can design the outcomes you want using the science of happiness and Power-Ups. By this point you'll know what to do as a Happy Leader. And you'll know why you're doing it. So we'll learn some tools and strategies to make it stick.

The truth is, the journey of the Happy Leader requires work. And that's because happiness requires work. Happiness doesn't come from knowledge alone. It comes from putting knowledge into action. So as you read, be ready to experiment, try things out and see what works best for you and your world.

HAPPY LEADERS PUT IN THE REPS.

Becoming a Happy Leader takes practice. But don't worry, I've built some reps right into the playbook for you. As you move through the book, you'll find simple exercises designed to help you try out new strategies or take a moment to pause and reflect on what you and your team might need. These exercises are woven throughout the book as **Action Shots** and **Happiness Huddles.**

ACTION SHOT ☆

Your moments to dive in and put ideas into practice. Whether it's trying a new habit, testing a Power-Up or shifting your perspective, these prompts are all about action. They're designed to help you experiment and discover what works best for you.

HAPPINESS HUDDLE ☺

Time to pause, reflect and connect the dots. These prompts give you space to think deeply, explore your insights and align your energy with what matters most.

THE PATH OF THE HAPPY LEADER IS WORTH IT.

Being a Happy Leader doesn't mean you won't face tough days. Embracing happiness as a leader won't erase challenges. But it will give you a toolkit to approach them with optimism, confidence and compassion. Happiness doesn't eliminate hardships—it transforms how you navigate them, helping you move forward from a place of strength and centeredness.

This path isn't easy. Breaking out of the old ways, rewriting what it means to be a leader—this takes courage. But this book is here to make that journey a little easier and to remind you that you're not alone. You're part of a community of people, showing up each day to lead with purpose and humanity, making a real difference in their lives and in the lives around them.

That's what being a Happy Leader is about. It's not a title—it's a way of living, leading and lifting others. And I can't wait to walk this path with you.

#TLDR: KEY TAKEAWAYS

1. **Happiness is a foundation for strong, meaningful leadership.** Leaders who embrace happiness cultivate environments where people flourish.

2. **Happiness can be intentionally designed into our lives and workplaces.** Leaders can create routines, spaces and relationships

that support happiness and inspire people to show up as their best selves.

3. **Happiness is a competitive advantage.** Leaders who prioritize happiness help people feel valued, productive and connected in ways that traditional, results-only models overlook.

ACTION SHOT ☆

Identify one activity or connection that energizes you each day. Building awareness around what brings you energy is a powerful first step in designing happiness intentionally.

HAPPINESS HUDDLE ☺

What's one aspect of your current environment that you could adjust to support greater happiness—for yourself and your team? Consider small tweaks that create more connection, focus or positivity.

Part 1:
Learn the Science

Discover the science of happiness in leadership, the Energy-Impact Model and The Eight Pillars of Happiness.

CHAPTER 1

Let's Talk About Happiness

"I realized that by focusing on what's positive and what could be, we unlock so much potential for change and growth."

– Melinda Gates

From ancient philosophers to modern researchers, humans have been fascinated by happiness for thousands of years—what it means, how to cultivate it and why it matters. Across centuries and cultures, this pursuit has touched on purpose, connection, fulfillment and well-being. In recent years, we've come to learn that happiness doesn't happen to us, but rather is an outcome and a lifestyle we can design for ourselves and others. It's a positive emotion that does way more that make us feel good–it fuels energy, engagement and impact in the world.

Today, happiness is seen as essential both for personal fulfillment and also for driving growth, creativity and resilience in workplaces and communities. Research is transforming our understanding of it, revealing practical strategies to support happiness in ways that benefit both individual people and the organizations they interact with. In short, we're moving beyond theory. We know that happiness is a powerful tool that helps us live and lead better and with more impact.

WHY DOES HAPPINESS MATTER IN LEADERSHIP, IN BUSINESS OR IN LIFE?

Because it leads to results. And impact.

As I've seen time and again—whether working with leaders, working for leaders or diving into the research itself—happiness is a game-changer. It fuels resilience, sharpens decision-making and enhances interpersonal relationships—all of which are essential for effective leadership.

But to be Happy Leaders, we need to understand why happiness leads to these results. When we grasp the science behind it, we can build the systems and environments that lead to both happier lives and higher-performing teams.

Happy Leaders foster qualities that help them engage meaningfully with others. They build trust, approach challenges with optimism and inspire confidence through their authenticity. Their teams, in turn, become more loyal, collaborative and innovative, creating a workplace culture where people feel empowered to contribute their best.

HAPPINESS HUDDLE ☺

Think of a leader who exemplifies happiness in action. What qualities or behaviors make them stand out? How does their happiness impact the people around them?

BUT THIS KNOWLEDGE ISN'T NEW.

It may feel like happiness is everywhere these days—in podcasts, books and even Yale's record-breaking course, *The Science of Well-Being.* But while this focus may feel new, the quest to understand happiness has ancient roots. Thinkers like Aristotle, Epicurus and many others devoted their lives to exploring what makes life fulfilling and their insights still shape our understanding today.

For both Aristotle and Epicurus, happiness was far more than a fleeting feeling. It was a way of living with purpose, simplicity and connection. Aristotle believed in aligning our actions with core values and pursuing a life of meaning. His focus on purpose-driven living resonates with today's leaders, who recognize the power of leading with values to inspire and engage their teams. Epicurus emphasized the importance of simplicity, peace and relationships, reminding us that happiness can be found in everyday moments and genuine connections.

These timeless ideas provide a foundation for leaders today: aligning values, building relationships and creating environments where people find meaning in both big goals and small moments. Happiness, as these philosophers saw it, is about designing a life that supports fulfillment— and that's a principle that will never go out of style.

♡

A BRIEF HISTORY OF THE STUDY OF HAPPINESS

The Buddha (c. 563–483 BCE) Taught that detachment from desires and practicing mindfulness leads to inner peace and freedom from suffering.

Socrates (470–399 BCE) Believed happiness came from self-knowledge and living virtuously. Examining life and acting morally were essential to flourishing.

Aristotle (384–322 BCE) Defined happiness (eudaimonia) as flourishing through reason and virtue. This required cultivating good habits and pursuing wisdom.

Epicurus (341–270 BCE) Saw happiness as stemming from simple pleasures, such as friendship, freedom and living without fear or pain.

Zeno of Citium (c. 334–262 BCE) Taught that happiness comes from aligning one's will with nature and focusing on what can be controlled, a cornerstone of Stoic philosophy.

Jesus of Nazareth (c. 4 BCE–30 CE) Taught that love, faith and service to others bring true fulfillment, emphasizing compassion, forgiveness and inner peace.

Jean-Jacques Rousseau (1712–1778 CE) Argued that happiness is found in living authentically and in harmony with nature, critiquing modern society for corrupting human contentment.

Jeremy Bentham (1748–1832 CE) Equated happiness with the greatest good for the greatest number. He viewed maximizing pleasure and minimizing pain as society's primary aim.

John Stuart Mill (1806–1873 CE) Emphasized that higher forms of happiness, such as intellectual and moral pleasures, were more valuable than simple pleasures.

Friedrich Nietzsche (1844–1900 CE) Saw happiness as a byproduct of embracing challenges, overcoming struggles and pursuing personal growth.

A BRIEF HISTORY OF THE STUDY OF HAPPINESS

Sigmund Freud (1856–1939 CE) Believed happiness came from balancing primal desires with societal expectations and achieving psychological harmony.

Albert Einstein (1879–1955 CE) Advocated for simplicity and meaningful relationships over material ambition, seeing calm and modest living as key to happiness.

Mihaly Csikszentmihalyi (1934–2021 CE) Introduced the concept of flow, suggesting that deep engagement in meaningful activities brings the greatest joy.

Martin Seligman (b. 1942 CE) Emphasizes well-being through meaning, relationships and accomplishment, framing happiness as the presence of flourishing rather than the absence of misery.

Dr. Barbara Fredrickson (b. 1964 CE) Teaches how positive emotions expand cognitive and social resources, enabling individuals to flourish over time.

Brené Brown (b. 1965 CE) Highlights the role of vulnerability and connection in happiness, emphasizing that courage and authenticity are essential to living a wholehearted life.

Dr. Sonja Lyubomirsky (b. 1966 CE) Focuses on how intentional activities like gratitude, kindness and positive thinking significantly impact long-term well-being.

Angela Duckworth (b. 1970 CE) Connects happiness to grit and perseverance, showing that passion and sustained effort are key drivers of well-being and personal fulfillment.

Dr. Laurie Santos (b. 1975 CE) Explores the cognitive biases that hinder happiness and offers science-backed strategies for cultivating joy.

$\heartsuit$

MODERN HAPPINESS EXPERTS ARE EXPANDING ON THESE ANCIENT IDEAS.

Today's happiness experts are building on these timeless insights, using research to explore what makes life meaningful. Their research brings new light and practical strategies that make happiness accessible and actionable for all.

Dr. Laurie Santos's work highlights simple daily practices—like gratitude, connection and valuing experiences over possessions—that nurture well-being[1]. Dr. Sonja Lyubomirsky's research shows that while genetics play a role, a significant portion of happiness is within our control, influenced by our choices and environment[2]. And Dr. Barbara Fredrickson reveals that positive emotions don't just feel good—they expand our mental resources, helping us build resilience and adaptability[3].

As a leader, these insights give you strategies that go beyond surface-level happiness and allow you to go much deeper to cultivate appreciation, foster connection and support well-being in meaningful ways. By focusing on intentional practices and creating a positive environment, you can design a culture where happiness fuels engagement, innovation and impact.

This is the work I do with leaders today—turning these insights into action. By integrating research-backed strategies into leadership and workplace culture, we create teams and communities where people feel empowered and ready to bring their best selves to every part of life. This is the work of a Happy Leader.

WE'RE WITNESSING A PROFOUND SHIFT IN HOW HAPPINESS IS UNDERSTOOD.

In my opinion, happiness is finally getting the attention it deserves when it comes to designing a world for human flourishing. The popularity of Yale's *The Science of Well-Being*—with millions of participants worldwide—reflects a deep desire to understand happiness on a more meaningful level. Companies are recognizing this shift too, with more leaders stepping into roles like Chief Happiness Officer to shape work environments centered on well-being and purpose. This collective focus shows that happiness is evolving, though slowly, from a personal pursuit to a shared value—something that strengthens both people and the organizations and communities they belong to.

You are part of this shift.

By creating spaces that foster happiness and human flourishing, you're helping shape a culture where everyone can contribute at their fullest. Because the future of happiness is about what we cultivate within ourselves *and* the environments we build for those around us. By taking this broader view, you're contributing to a world where happiness is woven into the very fabric of our workplaces and communities, laying a foundation for fulfillment and success that will last.

LET'S TAKE A CLOSER LOOK AT THE RESEARCH.

For much of the 20th century, psychology focused on treating dysfunction, addressing trauma and alleviating suffering. But in the 1990s, Dr. Martin Seligman wanted to go further and study what enables humans to flourish. This shift introduced a new question: *How do we help people build meaningful, fulfilling lives?*

The field of Positive Psychology that Seligman founded brought concepts like resilience, strengths and growth mindsets into the business world. Leaders now understand that cultivating happiness isn't just about preventing burnout—it's about creating workplaces where people can show up as their best selves for a common cause. This shift has led companies to focus more on well-being initiatives, integrating mindfulness programs, flexible work policies and strengths-based development to build cultures that support happiness and resilience.

Since its inception, Positive Psychology has shed light on what actually contributes to human flourishing (turns out it's not ping pong tables and unlimited PTO!). For you, this research isn't theoretical—it's a toolkit you can put to work to help you and your team thrive. These principles offer practical ways to build resilience and create meaningful connections. And when applied in leadership, they set the stage for a culture where people feel engaged, valued and motivated to contribute at their highest level.

Let's explore some core takeaways from Positive Psychology—insights that have profoundly shaped how the leaders I work with show up every day. In fact, understanding this research has completely transformed the way I show up in my own life, too. And that's why I'm sharing it with you here—because these principles are practical, powerful insights that can help you lead with greater confidence, connection and purpose.

KEY TAKEAWAYS FROM THE SCIENCE OF HAPPINESS

- ◇ Happiness is a multifaceted process.

- ◇ Living by our strengths increases fulfillment.

- ◇ Positive emotions help build resilience.

- ◇ Purpose and meaning are central to happiness.

- ◇ Human connection is foundational.

- ◇ Happiness is a learnable skill.

- ◇ Happiness is contagious.

HAPPINESS IS A MULTIFACETED PROCESS.

Happiness isn't a fleeting emotion. It's an active process shaped by our environment and behaviors. It's why there is no one state of happiness but instead a spectrum of positive and negative emotions that affect our energy and engagement. This understanding shifts the goal from simply "being happy" to actively creating more happiness or becoming happier. Recognizing that happiness is a process within our influence empowers us to cultivate it intentionally—in ourselves and within our teams. Leading with this awareness fosters accountability and encourages everyone to take ownership of their energy and happiness journey.

LIVING BY OUR STRENGTHS INCREASES FULFILLMENT.

Leveraging strengths is one of the most powerful ways to boost impact and effectiveness. Research shows that people who work from their strengths feel more confident, capable and satisfied. By recognizing and using your strengths—and helping your team members do the same—you create a strengths-based culture that's both supportive and productive. People are more likely to bring creativity, energy and a collaborative spirit when they're encouraged to use what they're naturally good at.

HAPPINESS HUDDLE ☺

Take a moment to identify your top three strengths. How can you integrate them more fully into your work this week? And how can you help team members do the same?

POSITIVE EMOTIONS HELP BUILD RESILIENCE.

Positive emotions are quite possibly the most powerful assets in your leadership toolkit. Dr. Barbara Fredrickson's Broaden and Build[4] theory shows that positive emotions do more than simply lift spirits in the moment—they expand our thinking, strengthen our relationships and build mental resilience. According to Fredrickson's research, when you and your team experience positive emotions like joy, gratitude or optimism, they broaden your perspectives, enabling you to see new possibilities, approach challenges creatively and deepen social bonds.

Positive emotions lay a foundation that helps your team handle adversity, fostering a culture where people feel supported, empowered and ready to face challenges. When you make space for happiness—whether by celebrating wins, sharing gratitude or encouraging team connections—you're helping fuel long-term success. And while we certainly cannot avoid challenges, we can lead with a mindset focused on growth, solutions and connection.

For Happy Leaders, this insight is invaluable—cultivating more positive energy equips you and your team to navigate difficulties with greater adaptability and resourcefulness.

PURPOSE AND MEANING ARE CENTRAL TO HAPPINESS.

People who feel connected to a purpose experience higher satisfaction, less stress and stronger resilience. For leaders, this means anchoring work in something deeper than daily tasks or targets. When you're clear on the "why" behind your efforts, it's easier to lead with conviction. It's easier to inspire your team. And it's easier to navigate challenges with a centered perspective. Leadership rooted in purpose and meaning helps your team see the value of their contributions, fostering a culture where everyone feels their work matters.

HUMAN CONNECTION IS FOUNDATIONAL TO HAPPINESS.

Relationships are everything because teams need trust and genuine connection to work at their best. Prioritizing human connection builds rapport and cohesion—essential for engagement and motivation. I've witnessed this time and time again in my work with leaders—when people feel seen and valued, they're more likely to collaborate and invest in the team's success. Simple actions, like taking time to recognize individual contributions or encouraging teammates to share something positive, can profoundly impact team culture. Authenticity and empathy build stronger bonds and create a team that feels unified and motivated.

ACTION SHOT ☆

Dedicate ten minutes in your next team meeting for everyone to share something they're grateful for that week. This simple exercise fosters connection and creates a positive, supportive team culture.

HAPPINESS PRACTICES ARE LEARNABLE SKILLS.

One of the most empowering insights from Positive Psychology is that happiness isn't fixed—it's a skill anyone can cultivate. Anyone.

Practices like mindfulness, gratitude and self-compassion can be intentionally developed, creating a toolbox for showing up at your best and empowering others to do the same. We have agency over this. We can get ourselves unstuck, practice happiness and create more of it in our lives. And just as importantly, we have the ability—and responsibility— to design systems and spaces that enable the people we lead to cultivate happiness for themselves.

Understanding happiness as a skill gives Happy Leaders tools to manage stress, make balanced decisions and maintain a positive presence that inspires and motivates. When you model these practices, you show your team that happiness is an accessible habit—not an abstract ideal. And that is game-changing.

HAPPINESS IS CONTAGIOUS.

Research shows that happiness spreads through communities and teams. Studies reveal that happiness has a ripple effect, increasing the likelihood of happiness among friends, family and coworkers[5]. When you intentionally create opportunities for happiness and model it for your team, you're not just elevating your own well-being—you're influencing others to feel and act more positively as well.

This phenomenon, known as the social network effect, shows that happiness moves through social networks up to three degrees. In other words, your happiness can positively affect your friends, your friends' friends and even their friends. It's a bit like the six degrees of Kevin Bacon game, but much more meaningful—and much faster.

Here's how happiness connects people–

- When someone becomes happy, their close friend's happiness is 25% more likely to increase.

- A spouse's likelihood of becoming happier rises by 8% when their partner experiences happiness.

- Happiness is contagious even next door, boosting a neighbor's happiness by 34%.

- A friend of a friend is nearly 10% more likely to feel happier when positive energy spreads through social ties.

- Even at three degrees of separation, happiness can travel—those loosely connected still have a 5.6% increased chance of becoming happier.

This proves that happiness isn't just a personal experience—it's a shared energy that shapes the way people engage and interact. Researchers found that 64% of people felt happier after reading positive posts on social media and studies suggest people share their positive experiences 70% of the time[6]. Think about the implications of that in the workplace! We have the power to design for spreading happiness.

We'll explore this concept more fully in the next chapter because it's that important, especially when it comes to leadership. Because happiness doesn't stop with you. When you practice and share it intentionally, you create environments where those around you are empowered to cultivate happiness for themselves too.

HAPPINESS IS A POWERFUL LEADERSHIP ADVANTAGE.

Understanding and prioritizing happiness is essential to effective leadership. Research shows that leaders who cultivate it within themselves and their teams experience higher engagement, greater resilience and increased innovation. When you model happiness, you create a culture where people feel valued and motivated to give their best. Leaders who understand the power of this build trust and psychological safety, allowing their team to better care for themselves and one other.

We've learned so much about happiness and human flourishing in the past thirty years. The insights can help you to lead with purpose and intentionality, creating a culture where positive emotions and productivity reinforce one another. It shifts leadership from driving results to building a team that works together, innovates together and succeeds together.

While there is a lot of happiness research out there and available to us these days, a majority of it centers on personal mindset and individual practices, suggesting that happiness is something you create within yourself—through your attitudes, habits and outlook on life. But as we've just learned, happiness is bigger than me and you. So yes, it's true that each of us plays a role in our own happiness. But there's a critical element that often gets overlooked–the power of our environment. Your workplace, community and relationships shape your happiness in ways that can either uplift or undermine even your best efforts.

In her book *The How of Happiness*, Dr. Sonja Lyubomirsky introduces the Happiness Pie to explain what influences happiness[7]. According to her research, about 50% of happiness is influenced by genetics, 40% by intentional activities and only 10% by external circumstances, including our environment. While 10% may seem small, even small shifts in environmental conditions can have a ripple effect on happiness. Studies show that our surroundings significantly impact our ability to sustain positive mindset practices. For example, a toxic work culture can undermine even the most optimistic outlook, while a supportive, inclusive environment can elevate everyone's resilience and engagement.

Imagine the difference when we shift the focus beyond personal happiness to include the spaces and systems we create around us. When you intentionally design environments that support positive emotions, you're not only setting yourself up for sustainable happiness but you are also creating a foundation for everyone you lead. Leaders who understand the communal aspects of happiness—trust, inclusivity and psychological safety—build cultures where people feel valued, supported and motivated to bring their best every day.

HAPPINESS HUDDLE ☺

How does your current environment support or hinder happiness for you and your team? What's one way you could create a more positive space this week?

HAPPIER SPACES BENEFIT EVERYONE.

Think of someone who's dedicated to practicing gratitude, and mindfulness every day. They're doing all the right things for personal happiness, yet if they walk into a toxic workplace, much of their hard work is undone. Environments that aren't supportive can counteract even the strongest mindsets. That's because happiness, we now know, is shaped by our communities, workplaces and cultures.

This is where many conversations on happiness stop. This is why happiness-focused leadership is so different from what's out there now. Because the current focus is almost exclusively on personal practices—access to wellness programs and meditation apps—without acknowledging our shared responsibility to design spaces that enable happiness for others. What good is a gym membership if employees don't have the time or freedom to use it?

Sustainable happiness is both personal and communal. And we each have a role in cultivating our own happiness and in creating environments where happiness can flourish for those around us.

Let's take a look at this in action.

PATAGONIA PROVES THAT HAPPINESS IS A SERIOUS BUSINESS ADVANTAGE.

Patagonia's mission is all about purpose—build the best product, cause no unnecessary harm and use business to inspire solutions to the environmental crisis.

This purpose-driven approach aligns happiness and impact, creating a culture where people feel their work has real meaning. As founder Yvon Chouinard explains in Let My People Go Surfing, the company's commitment to values is central to its business strategy, creating an environment where people feel empowered to bring their whole selves to work[8].

Living It: Patagonia walks the talk with initiatives like onsite childcare, flexible schedules, paid volunteer days and support for environmental activism. These aren't simply perks. They are intentional choices that let employees balance life and work while contributing to something bigger than themselves.

Impact: Patagonia's focus on employee happiness and well-being drives impressive business results. With high employee retention, strong loyalty and a dedicated customer base, Patagonia shows us that when people feel supported, business thrives. Happiness and purpose are powerful tools for growth.

HAPPIER COMPANIES ARE MORE SUCCESSFUL.

Studies reveal a powerful connection between happiness and organizational success. Happier companies—those that intentionally foster wellbeing and prioritize employee happiness—don't just perform better but also enjoy greater innovation, faster growth and significantly higher retention rates. For leaders like you, this is a business strategy with tangible outcomes. When employees feel valued, supported and genuinely happy at work, they bring a level of energy, engagement and commitment that positively impacts every part of the organization.

Recent research highlights the strong link between employee wellbeing and financial success. Companies ranked in the top 100 for employee wellbeing consistently outperform major stock market indices like the Dow Jones and S&P 500. This demonstrates that prioritizing employee wellbeing not only leads to higher financial returns but also reinforces the strategic value of investing in workplace happiness[9].

Key findings from the research include—

- Companies with high employee wellbeing scores tend to achieve higher market valuations and stronger return on assets compared to their peers.

- Positive work environments that focus on wellbeing lead to increased productivity, reduced turnover and enhanced overall performance.

- Portfolios of top wellbeing companies have outperformed both the S&P 500 and Dow Jones over defined periods, showcasing the sustained financial benefits of prioritizing employee wellbeing.

Top 100 by Work Wellbeing Score

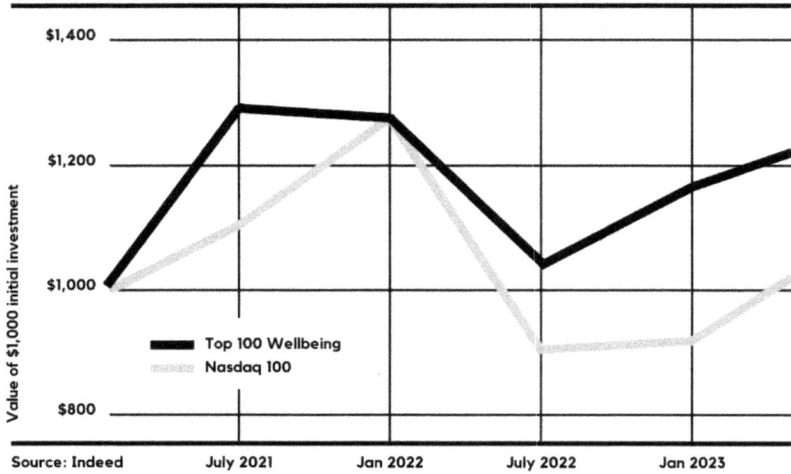

Companies leading in work well-being outperform the S&P 500, Dow Jones, and Nasdaq 100, showing that prioritizing employee happiness fuels financial success.
(Source: Indeed)

The good news is that implementing happiness practices doesn't require a major overhaul or an extravagant budget. Even in fast-paced settings, my clients have seen how small actions—like starting meetings with a round of appreciation or taking a few minutes each week to check in with team members—can significantly boost morale, communication and trust. These quick practices help prevent burnout and create a culture of support, equipping your team to handle challenges with resilience.

By making space for employee happiness, even when time is tight, you're positioning your team for success.

WORKPLACE HAPPINESS IS MEASURABLE.

And as we've seen, the ROI speaks for itself. Fostering happiness at work leads to outcomes that are both measurable and meaningful. Companies that prioritize employee happiness see higher engagement, with employees more motivated, focused and connected to their work. Increased happiness also fuels innovation, as employees in positive environments are more creative, open to new ideas and willing to take thoughtful risks.

When I work with clients, we start by benchmarking with a 24-point assessment that provides a detailed snapshot of workplace happiness and its effects on productivity, engagement and innovation. This baseline data identifies opportunities for improvement and serves as a foundation for tracking progress over time. Repeating the assessment during implementation helps monitor where improvements are happening and fine-tune strategies for even greater impact.

Key metrics—like engagement scores, retention rates, absenteeism and productivity—offer additional insights into how initiatives are performing. A reduction in turnover or an increase in job satisfaction signals progress, while regular team surveys provide direct feedback to refine your approach along the way.

Let's be clear—happiness-focused leadership isn't about promoting constant positivity. It's about fostering resilience and adaptability. It's about increased creativity and collaboration. It's about supporting one another to show up fully and contribute meaningfully every day. Happier teams are more motivated, collaborative and better equipped to sustain productivity under pressure.

By integrating happiness practices and tracking their effects, you're building a culture that supports both your people and the performance needed for success. Traditional management models often prioritize efficiency and measurable output, but leaders who embrace the science of happiness understand that happiness and productivity go hand in hand. Happy leadership empowers companies to shift toward cultures of creativity and collaboration, proving that happiness and performance grow stronger together.

ACTION SHOT ☆

Identify one area in your team where well-being could be improved. Consider experimenting with flexible work hours, acknowledgment practices or supportive check-ins to see how a small change in environment impacts team morale.

Happy leadership directly impacts the bottom line. When you prioritize employee well-being, you're setting up your team—and your organization—for greater success. Research consistently shows that companies with higher levels of employee happiness and engagement outperform their peers financially, with benefits that range from increased productivity to stronger retention. In one study, happy employees were found to be 12% more productive, while unhappy employees were 10% less productive[10]. For you, this productivity boost means higher revenue, better customer service and greater profitability across your team.

By creating a workplace where people feel energized and engaged, you're reducing burnout, absenteeism and lowering turnover. According to Gallup, organizations with engaged, happy employees see a 41% reduction in absenteeism and a 17% increase in productivity[11]. When employees feel appreciated, they're more likely to stay and grow within the organization, saving you from costly turnover and recruitment cycles and fostering a team that's committed to your shared mission.

Your commitment to happiness also strengthens your company's reputation. Today's workforce is increasingly drawn to companies that demonstrate genuine care for their people. When you invest in them, you're positioning your company as forward-thinking and human-centered—a competitive advantage that attracts both top talent and loyal customers.

And let's not overlook the impact of psychological safety on business success. Google's Project Aristotle study found that psychological safety—the sense that it's safe to take risks and share ideas without fear of judgment—was the most crucial factor in team success12. When you foster a culture of mutual trust and respect, you're encouraging open collaboration and innovation, creating an environment where happiness and productivity naturally reinforce each other.

In short, happier companies—like the one you're helping to lead—operate with resilience, foster innovation and attract people who are inspired to bring their best every day. In an era where employees prioritize meaning and fulfillment, being a Happy Leader is one of the most powerful strategies for creating sustainable success.

HAPPINESS IS A SHARED RESPONSIBILITY.

By now you know that happiness goes beyond an individual. It involves designing systems and spaces that support it on a communal level. As we move forward in this book, we'll explore how to cultivate happiness within ourselves and in the spaces we influence, using The Energy-Impact Model and The Eight Pillars of Happiness to supercharge your team and life.

When happiness becomes a core part of your leadership, you will drive positive energy, engagement and impact. In today's market, these outcomes are essential. Leaders who design for happiness create cultures where people feel valued, inspired and motivated to bring their best selves to work. Happiness is the foundation of visionary leadership, enabling you to meet today's challenges with science and intentional action.

Happiness leads to both a meaningful life and successful leadership. And it's time we design with it in mind—not just for ourselves but for the world around us.

In the next chapter we'll dive into energy—why it matters and how it shapes the world around us, both at work and at home. You'll discover the Energy-Impact Model, a powerful tool that helps you design your environment for greater engagement and impact. You'll gain a clear understanding of how energy influences everything and, most importantly, how to harness it to create the results you want.

#TLDR: KEY TAKEAWAYS

1. **Happiness is a skill.** Happiness isn't a fleeting feeling—it's a learnable skill that fuels energy, engagement and impact.

2. **Happiness is contagious.** It spreads through relationships and social networks, influencing friends, coworkers and communities.

3. **Happiness drives business success.** Organizations that prioritize employee happiness achieve higher engagement, productivity and retention—outperforming major stock indices and strengthening their competitive edge.

ACTION SHOT ☆

Identify one happiness practice to try this week, such as gratitude journaling, reflecting on your strengths or connecting with someone who brings you joy. Start small and notice how it influences your day.

HAPPINESS HUDDLE ☺

How much of your happiness do you believe is within your control?
How can you contribute to the happiness of those around you?

CHAPTER 2

Leading with Energy

*"You are responsible for the energy you bring into the room.
When we lead with joy, we create space for others to do the same."*
—Oprah Winfrey

Energy is everything.

It's a saying you've probably heard, maybe even rolled your eyes at once or twice. It can sound abstract or out of place in a business setting. But as a leader, you know there's nothing vague about energy. Science backs it up, but more importantly, so does experience. And happiness? It's a core part of this positive energy—an essential source that fuels creativity, collaboration and resilience.

The truth is, this idea goes far beyond formal business leadership—it applies to all forms of leadership, whether you're the president of a country, a team lead at a small start-up or a parent running a busy household. Energy radiates outward, influencing engagement and outcomes in every environment. Imagine a national leader whose positive, uplifting energy inspires unity and hope across millions of people. Now think of a parent whose steady, encouraging energy fosters confidence, curiosity and trust in their children. Each of these leaders, in their own space, shapes the lives of those around them.

So wherever you fall on the leadership spectrum, this is for you. Because leadership isn't a title–it's a way of navigating your world with influence. And by understanding and nurturing positive energy—including happiness—you'll discover that you can amplify your impact with everyone around you.

Think about it. Have you ever had one of those weeks (or months, or years) where everything just seemed to click? You were landing clients or projects with ease, making headway on all your goals and solving problems as quickly as they came up. You were in flow, and so was everyone around you. This wasn't luck. It was momentum—positive energy in action.

And we've all been on the other side, too. Times when every little thing seemed to drag on. No matter how hard you worked, it felt like moving through quicksand and no one around you seemed to have a spark, either. This is the other side of energy, the drain that pulls you and your team down.

Just as positive personal energy fuels engagement and impact, low or negative energy does the opposite. When your energy is low—due to stress, burnout or negativity—your engagement with others weakens, creativity fades and your impact diminishes. In leadership, that low energy can spread quickly, affecting the mood, morale and productivity of your entire team.

My goal for you in this chapter is to help you tap into and generate more of that positive, flowing energy. And to do that, we'll be walking through the Energy-Impact Model—a framework designed to show you how personal energy drives engagement and, ultimately, impact. Because when you bring positive energy into your work, you bring it to your team. And that impacts everything.

ENERGY IS THE HEARTBEAT OF LEADERSHIP.

Every action, thought and decision you make radiates energy that influences not only you but also each person on your team. When both you and your team members cultivate positive energy, it creates a shared momentum that boosts morale, engagement and productivity across the board.

But it's not just about the energy itself. It's about the type of energy you bring to your leadership. In the same way that positive energy can build momentum and inspire, negative energy drains morale and motivation, and often much faster than we realize.

Positive leadership energy sustains teams through both periods of momentum and times of change, such as restructuring or other challenging phases. During these moments, your energy helps stabilize the team, encouraging resilience, focus and resourcefulness even when conditions are tough. By leading with confidence and optimism, you create a supportive environment that fosters adaptability and trust—even when outcomes aren't guaranteed.

Let's bring this concept to life by breaking down how different leadership styles either elevate or erode energy within teams. As you read through each leadership style, see if any feel familiar from your own experience—either in your leadership journey or in leaders you've worked with.

LEADERSHIP STYLES THAT DEPLETE ENERGY.

Each leader highlighted below brings specific traits and intentions to their role, but their energy can sometimes lead to unintended consequences for themselves and their teams.

HYPER-INDEPENDENT HENRY

Henry believes that to be a strong leader, he has to handle everything on his own. He's incredibly driven and sets high standards, working late rather than asking for help and rarely sharing his workload because he's convinced no one else can meet his expectations. For Henry, independence is strength and relying on others feels risky.

The downside? Henry's team feels shut out and undervalued. They want to support him and contribute, but he rarely lets them in. As a result, they operate in silos, often feeling disconnected from each other and from Henry's vision. Henry, meanwhile, is exhausted. Despite his best intentions, his hyper-independence is creating a cycle of burnout—for him and his team.

FEAR-FOCUSED FIONA

Fiona's vigilance and her eye for risk helps her team avoid mistakes that others might miss. She's always anticipating the next potential issue, quick to point out what could go wrong. Her motto is "better safe than sorry," and she genuinely believes her caution is protecting the team.

But Fiona's constant focus on worst-case scenarios holds her team back. Team members hesitate to share ideas or take risks, fearing that Fiona's feedback will focus on all the ways it might fail. Instead of feeling empowered, they grow more risk-averse and cautious, held back by Fiona's fear-driven approach. Though her intentions are protective, Fiona's leadership limits growth and creates a high-stress environment where innovation is stifled.

PERFECTIONIST PATRICK

Patrick takes pride in maintaining high standards and his attention to detail ensures the team delivers quality work. He believes his hands-on approach is essential to success, regularly checking in, tweaking projects and getting involved in the details to make sure everything's just right. Patrick's dedication to excellence is well-intentioned, but his need for control can weigh down his team.

Under Patrick's constant oversight, team members feel stifled and demoralized. They feel they don't have ownership of their work, knowing that Patrick will adjust it anyway. Over time, his micromanagement erodes their confidence and motivation. Instead of fostering high performance, Patrick's perfectionism leads to a disengaged team that's afraid to make mistakes or take initiative.

DISCONNECTED DANA

Dana is focused on efficiency and results, ensuring tasks get done and deadlines are met. She views work relationships in terms of output and tends to keep personal interactions to a minimum, preferring a "strictly business" demeanor. Dana believes that a professional distance keeps things objective and avoids unnecessary distractions.

However, Dana's team feels more like tools than people. They do their jobs, but they don't feel connected to each other—or to Dana. This lack of personal engagement makes them feel undervalued and disconnected, reducing morale and trust. Without a sense of camaraderie or personal connection, Dana's team lacks cohesion and loyalty, often leaving them without the trust and engagement needed for long-term success.

EGO-DRIVEN ED

Ed thrives on recognition and personal success. He's motivated by ambitious goals and thrives on being seen as the star of the team, often positioning himself in the spotlight and ensuring others notice his contributions. His drive and confidence help him reach goals and push the team forward, but his focus on personal achievement has a negative impact.

Unfortunately, Ed's self-centered style can quickly turn toxic. His team often feels overlooked, as their contributions are minimized or ignored. Ed's need for recognition stirs competition rather than collaboration, and team members start to feel like rivals rather than allies. Instead of a supportive environment, Ed's team grows resentful and trust erodes as people become increasingly frustrated by his ego-driven style.

PASSIVE PETE

Pete is laid-back and easygoing, which helps keep his team's stress levels low. He believes in giving people space and avoids getting involved in the details, trusting his team to get things done. However, Pete's approach sometimes turns into indifference. He's not fully present in decision-making, leaving things up to his team but without a clear sense of direction or guidance.

Pete's team often feels adrift, unsure of priorities and disconnected from a shared vision. Without clear guidance or direction, they struggle to maintain momentum and energy. While Pete's hands-off style avoids creating direct stress, it leaves his team feeling complacent and uninspired. The lack of active leadership translates into a lack of purpose, causing team spirit and engagement to gradually erode.

$$\heartsuit$$

These examples may feel familiar. Each of these leaders, in their own way, unintentionally drains team energy and morale. Their intentions may be good, but the energy they bring to their leadership style has real, tangible effects on team trust, productivity and motivation. This is a powerful reminder that as leaders, the energy we bring directly shapes the team dynamics and outcomes around us.

HAPPINESS HUDDLE ☺

Do any of these styles resonate with your own leadership experiences? Where might you see opportunities to shift energy dynamics?

THERE IS ANOTHER WAY TO LEAD.

Luckily, you and I—and science—know there's a better way. Leaders don't have to bear the weight of every challenge alone or feel stretched thin by endless demands. They don't need to motivate through fear or keep a strict distance to maintain control. Instead, they can lead in a way that supports both themselves and their teams—creating an environment that lifts everyone involved. It's an approach that fuels positive energy, engagement and lasting impact. This is the path of the Happy Leader.

A Happy Leader doesn't just know that people perform better when they're energized and engaged—they live it, and it shows in every interaction. Happy Leaders believe that personal well-being is an essential part of sustaining team performance and growth. They understand that work and life aren't two separate silos–they're interconnected. When people feel good at work, that positivity carries into other areas of their lives. And when people feel valued in their lives, they bring that energy back into work. For the Happy Leader, this isn't wishful thinking—it's the foundation of their leadership.

This positive energy is shared through everyday interactions and it becomes a powerful resource during challenges. The Happy Leader's energy doesn't waver when the going gets tough. In challenging times— whether through organizational changes, tight deadlines or unexpected setbacks—their resilience and optimism serve as a steadying force, providing their team with clarity and confidence to face obstacles. For the Happy Leader, optimism is a core trait that empowers the team to tackle difficulties with confidence and optimism.

So how does a Happy Leader show up? Picture someone who listens deeply, takes the time to understand their team and creates a space where ideas flow freely. They're steady, authentic and present, greeting challenges with curiosity and optimism rather than frustration or fear. Happy Leaders foster psychological safety, making it clear that mistakes are part of growth and that everyone's voice matters. In meetings, they're the first to celebrate wins—both big and small—and they encourage others to do the same.

Happy Leaders delegate with trust. They believe in their team's abilities and aren't afraid to step back, allowing team members to take ownership, learn and even struggle a bit. They recognize that autonomy fuels growth and that growth fuels engagement. A Happy Leader sets clear goals but leaves plenty of room for creative freedom, inspiring their team to bring their best ideas and strengths forward. And when challenges arise, they don't rush to control every detail. Instead, they collaborate, focusing on solutions and remaining calm, modeling resilience and adaptability.

This approach impacts the work, the team and the outcome. The Happy Leader's positive energy is a catalyst, inspiring each team member to cultivate their own sense of optimism, purpose and engagement. When each person on the team brings their best energy to work, the entire group benefits, creating a positive feedback loop of shared enthusiasm and support. Team members feel seen and respected, and in turn, they show up with greater energy and commitment.

A team led by a Happy Leader isn't just productive—they're engaged and innovative. When challenges come, they know they'll be met with encouragement rather than criticism. They're empowered to take risks, push boundaries and support one another. This team is more than a collection of people, roles and titles–they're a unit, working together with shared purpose and trust.

As we'll see in the Energy-Impact Model, a Happy Leader's positive energy not only boosts their own impact but spreads throughout their entire team, creating a culture of engagement, performance and impact.

HOW POSITIVE ENERGY FUELS EXTRAORDINARY IMPACT.

Now that we've seen how energy plays out in different leadership styles, let's break down the science behind it. Because energy isn't a fluffy, feel-good concept—it's a science-backed, evidence-based approach to creating the positive energy that fuels real, lasting impact.

The Energy-Impact Model is a framework I designed to show the relationship between personal happiness and the effect it creates throughout people, projects and teams. Personal energy is at the center, with each team member acting as a unique energy source that radiates outward, influencing everything and everyone it touches. When everyone on a team—including you—is living in positive energy, it creates a collective vitality that supports productivity, collaboration and creativity.

The model is built around three interconnected levels: personal energy, engagement and impact. As positive energy grows at the personal level, it naturally fosters higher engagement and deeper connections. This, in turn, strengthens team culture and drives greater impact on work, customers and the organization as a whole—creating an energetic cycle of successful outcomes.

Picture yourself as the central energy source, with every action you take radiating outward to influence those around you. By nurturing your energy, you enhance engagement and amplify impact, shaping a culture of positivity and high performance across your team and organization.

Let's break down each level of the model to see how it can transform the way you and your team approach work, life and everything in-between.

Energy-Impact Model

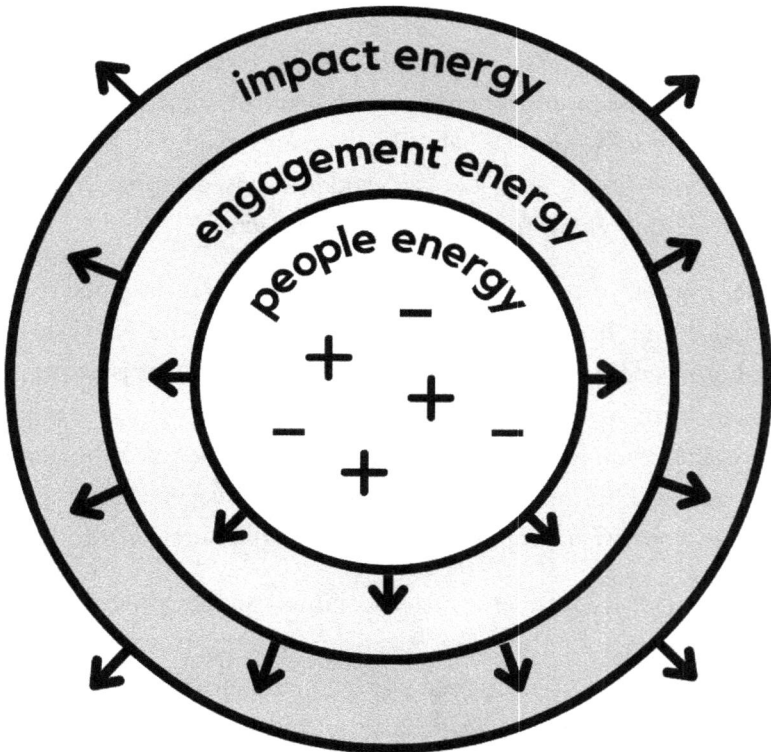

The Energy-Impact Model shows how personal energy fuels engagement, driving collaboration and transforming that momentum into measurable impact.

YOUR PERSONAL ENERGY IS THE CORE OF POSITIVE IMPACT.

At the heart of the Energy-Impact Model is personal energy—the inner wellspring of happiness and positive energy that you cultivate within yourself. This is essential for leaders because positive personal energy fuels everything else you do. And building this energy is grounded in intentional practices.

As we learned in the previous chapter, cultivating happiness has powerful, measurable effects on energy and overall well-being. The *Happiness Advantage* by Shawn Achor highlights that positive emotions activate the brain in ways that lead to higher energy levels, increased resilience and better problem-solving abilities[13].

To create and sustain positive energy, we can turn to my framework, The Eight Pillars of Happiness. Each of these science-backed pillars creates the positive energy that supports personal flourishing for you as a leader and for every member of your team. When each person practices and lives these pillars, they bring their best energy to work, building an engaged and high-performing team culture.

We'll do a deep dive into each of these pillars in the next chapter, but for now know that they are the skillsets that create personal positive energy.

The benefits of strengthening these pillars extend far beyond work. Positive energy practices are life skills that enhance relationships, reduce stress and build personal resilience. For example, research from Dr. Martin Seligman shows that daily gratitude practices lead to lasting improvements in emotional well-being and resilience, positively influencing health, stress levels and personal connections[14].

THE EIGHT PILLARS OF HAPPINESS	
Confidence	Believing in one's abilities and potential.
Authenticity	Being true to oneself and aligning actions with values.
Purpose	Having a sense of meaning and direction.
Compassion	Showing kindness and grace to oneself and others.
Gratitude	Recognizing and appreciating positive aspects of life.
Curiosity	Seeking new experiences and learning opportunities.
Optimism	Focusing on positive outcomes and possibilities.
Feeling	Being attuned to and expressing emotions in healthy ways.

It's important to remember that energy flows both ways. When we neglect The Eight Pillars, our energy suffers. And when your energy is low, engagement weakens, creativity fades and impact diminishes. In leadership, energy spreads quickly—whether high or low—affecting your team's mood, morale and productivity.

By strengthening these pillars, you can proactively design your happiness, allowing you to show up in work and life with more positive energy. This personal energy doesn't just stay within you—it flows into the next level of the model, boosting your engagement with the people and projects that matter most.

ENGAGEMENT CONNECTS YOU WITH PEOPLE, PROJECTS AND COMMUNITIES.

The middle ring of the Energy-Impact Model represents engagement—the active connection you have with others, your work and your community. When personal energy is strong, it naturally extends outward, creating positive engagement in relationships and projects. But engagement is about more than showing up. It's about being fully present, collaborative and invested when you do. Leaders with high levels of positive engagement foster cultures of trust, open communication and psychological safety— all essential for driving team productivity and performance.

At work, positive engagement leads to better collaboration, higher job satisfaction and stronger commitment to shared goals. According to a study by Gallup, highly engaged teams are 17% more productive, 21% more profitable and experience significantly lower turnover than teams with low engagement15. Engaged team members consistently bring their best, which elevates the entire organization's potential.

> A leader's personal energy directly influences engagement. For example, leaders who practice compassion and gratitude often foster more collaborative environments. Research from the Greater Good Science Center at UC Berkeley shows that when people feel valued and supported, they're more likely to contribute ideas, take creative risks and engage meaningfully.[16]

Let's play this out. Imagine making a deliberate effort to acknowledge and celebrate each team member's contributions in meetings. This simple practice of gratitude boosts your personal energy and creates a more inclusive, positive atmosphere. Team members feel seen, respected and motivated, increasing their engagement and inspiring them to bring new ideas forward.

This is where personal energy transforms into outward engagement, lifting up everyone involved. And like the inner ring of the model, the middle ring isn't limited to the workplace. Engagement also includes family, friendships and community involvement. When you're fully engaged, you can make meaningful contributions to the people and places that matter most

POSITIVE ENERGY AND ENGAGEMENT CREATE IMPACT.

The outer ring of the model represents impact—the collective effect that positive energy and engagement have on broader outcomes. When leaders cultivate personal energy and foster positive engagement, it inevitably leads to measurable, meaningful impact across their teams, their organizations and their communities. This outer ring is where positive workplace culture becomes a competitive advantage, driving higher productivity, stronger collaboration and financial success.

Outside the workplace, the impact of this model extends into communities and personal relationships. Studies show that people who experience positive interactions and environments are more likely to volunteer, engage civically and form stronger bonds in their personal lives[17]. This is what it means to make a lasting impact–intentionally designing a world where happiness and collaboration create a positive feedback loop that builds on itself over time.

Think back to Patagonia—by prioritizing happiness and shared purpose, the company has created a work culture where positive energy radiates from leadership to employees and outward to their customers. This values-driven approach supports well-being, collaboration and business success, illustrating how the Energy-Impact Model works in real life.

As we can see, positive energy at the personal level fuels meaningful engagement, which grows to create real-world impact. The Energy-

Impact Model shows that by cultivating happiness within ourselves, we set the stage for engagement that inspires and impacts everyone we interact with.

ENERGY BEYOND THE OFFICE WALLS.

One of the most powerful aspects of the Energy-Impact Model is its versatility. While we often imagine the leader as the central source of energy, the model can be applied in virtually any setting, with any person at the center. Whether it's a team member, a customer, a family member or even a neighbor, everyone's positive energy spreads outward, creating engagement and impact in ways that shape the world.

Consider how this plays out with a customer as the central energy source. Let's say a customer is delighted by your product. Their positive energy drives them to engage more deeply with your brand, leading to loyalty and a long-term relationship. Over time, this happy customer recommends your brand to friends, shares positive reviews online and becomes a repeat buyer. The impact? Higher customer retention, stronger brand reputation and increased lifetime value—all sparked by that customer's initial positive experience.

Now let's move closer to home. Imagine applying this model in your personal life, with your partner as the central energy source. When your partner feels valued and appreciated, their happiness grows. That positive energy then flows into your relationship, leading to more meaningful conversations, greater support and a stronger overall connection. This energy then extends to your children and to your work life. Just like in the workplace, the impact of positive personal energy radiates outward, creating engagement and impact beyond that initial person.

In each of these cases, the model shows that positive energy doesn't just influence immediate interactions—it creates lasting value. Whether at home or in the office, when each person actively nurtures their energy, they fuel engagement and impact in a way that reinforces happiness for everyone. This is the strength of the Energy-Impact Model—it's a framework you can apply in any area of life, enabling you to create meaningful impact wherever you go.

HARNESS THIS MODEL TO LEAD WITH POSITIVE ENERGY.

The Energy-Impact Model is a roadmap for embodying the qualities of a Happy Leader. By consciously nurturing each level of this model, you're equipping yourself to foster meaningful engagement and drive impact that resonates far beyond yourself.

When you prioritize your personal energy, you're filling the well that fuels your happiness, motivation and productivity. As this energy flows outward into engagement, you're not just leading by example—you're intentionally designing an environment that supports your team's energy as well. By creating structures, routines and spaces that foster this positive energy, you enable each team member to cultivate their own energy, engagement and impact. This strengthens both individual and team success, ensuring sustainable performance and a positive workplace culture.

This is the way of the Happy Leader—where positive energy and effectiveness go hand in hand. As you invest in yourself, you're both enhancing your leadership and empowering everyone around you.

In the next chapter we'll explore The Eight Pillars of Happiness, the foundation for your personal energy, setting the stage for meaningful engagement and lasting impact. By strengthening these pillars, you're equipping yourself with the energy you need each day—fueling both your leadership and the collective energy of your entire team.

#TLDR: KEY TAKEAWAYS

1. **Energy fuels impact.** The Energy-Impact Model shows that a leader's energy directly shapes team engagement and productivity, driving meaningful results.

2. **You are in charge of your impact.** By nurturing personal energy, leaders foster positive engagement and lasting impact, making happiness a powerful leadership strategy.

3. **Low energy comes at a high cost.** Just as positive energy fuels engagement, low energy drains morale and effectiveness. Prioritizing well-being is essential for building a resilient, thriving culture.

ACTION SHOT ☆

Identify one practice to boost your personal energy this week. Notice how it affects your mood and energy in both work and life.

HAPPINESS HUDDLE ☺

Consider the current energy you're bringing to your leadership. How does it impact your team, and how could a focus on positive personal energy enhance your team's engagement and outcomes?

CHAPTER 3

The Eight Pillars of Happiness

"My mission in life is not merely to survive, but to thrive; and to do so with some passion, some compassion, some humor, and some style."

— Maya Angelou

You've already started to see how happiness shapes your energy and your leadership. Now I'm excited to share a framework that can take everything you've learned and make it tangible, actionable and truly life-changing. The Eight Pillars of Happiness are the foundation of everything I teach. And for good reason—they work.

This framework isn't a theory. It's the secret sauce I've shared with leaders, teams and friends around my own kitchen table for almost a decade. The Eight Pillars fuel your personal energy, help you bounce back through challenges and create sustainable happiness in your life. They're at the heart of the Energy-Impact Model because they drive the energy that connects everything and everyone around you.

The best part? They don't require expensive tools or elaborate plans. They're built into you already, waiting to be strengthened and used. So whether you're looking to deepen your relationships, bring more creativity to your work or simply feel more energized and balanced, the Eight Pillars show you how to design happiness for yourself and for those you lead.

This is how we intentionally choose to live and lead with happiness. This is the secret to being a Happy Leader.

Think of the Eight Pillars as the foundational skills for positive energy. Just as an athlete practices moves and techniques to improve their performance, you can build happiness by practicing the skills that make it possible. If you wanted to become a better basketball player, you'd work on your shooting, footwork and endurance. You wouldn't expect to become skilled overnight—you'd understand that it takes time and intentional practice. The Eight Pillars work in much the same way. Each pillar strengthens your foundation, making positive energy easier to access and sustain over time.

These pillars emerged from my own search to understand and experience happiness more fully. I immersed myself in books, research and insights from experts across fields—each offering a perspective on what it means to live a fulfilling life. Eight key attributes showed up over and over again as essential elements of human flourishing. Over time I began aligning my life (and my family's) around them. And as I practiced these different skills, I discovered they led to a real, energy-based sense of happiness—not only as a person, but as a parent, partner and leader.

For a decade now, I've been practicing these skills to intentionally design the energy I want more of in my life and relationships. And the ROI has been bigger and better than I ever imagined. That's why I now dedicate my time and energy to sharing this framework with others—because we deserve more.

As people navigating an interconnected world, we deserve to do so with positive engagement and meaningful impact. The Eight Pillars of Happiness provide the framework for designing a world where human flourishing is possible. As Happy Leaders, it's our responsibility to initiate that change, embrace the science and create workspaces that empower our teams to show up at their best every day.

And that's the key here. Because beyond your personal happiness—which is super important and I so want that for you!—the Eight Pillars will help you design environments where others can flourish too. As you bring these skills into your life as a Happy Leader, you're building the foundation for your team and organization to grow. This is what sets a Happy Leader apart—your happiness becomes a source of inspiration and support that impacts your relationships, your team and your community.

It's important to understand that these pillars aren't meant to be followed in any set order and there's no hierarchy. Some may feel intuitive to you, while others may invite you to stretch beyond your comfort zone. In this chapter, we'll explore each of them, reflecting on why they matter, the practical benefits of them and how to start building them into your day-to-day life.

We'll begin with Confidence, a pillar rooted in trusting yourself and your abilities, even when faced with uncertainty. Confidence is knowing that, no matter the situation, you have access to what you need to succeed. Let's get started.

CONFIDENCE

Confidence is often misunderstood. Many assume it means always having the right answers, knowing the most or being the best. But that isn't Confidence at all—it's a myth that leads to unnecessary pressure and self-doubt. True Confidence, as a pillar of happiness, is much more empowering and grounded.

Confidence is about believing in your abilities and potential.

Confidence is about believing in your abilities and potential. It's cultivating a deep trust in yourself and your resources, even when outcomes are uncertain. It's not about always knowing what to do. Rather it's about trusting that you can figure it out, access the tools you need or learn along the way. This perspective shifts Confidence from being a fixed trait to a learnable skill that grows with practice.

Confident leaders don't need all the answers. Instead, they approach challenges with curiosity and a willingness to learn, showing their team that adaptability and growth matter more than perfection. By redefining Confidence in this way, you create a work culture where people feel empowered to take risks, embrace challenges and celebrate progress.

CONFIDENCE QUICK FACTS

◇ **Boosts performance**. Self-efficacy—the belief in one's ability to succeed—is linked to higher motivation, resilience and emotional well-being.

◇ **Creates psychological safety**. Confidence fosters environments where people feel safe to take risks, share ideas and trust one another, creating the foundation for collaboration and innovation.

◇ **Strengthens decision-making**. Confidence empowers people to make assertive choices while staying open to feedback, balancing momentum with adaptability in changing situations.

◇ **Inspires others**. Modeling trust in yourself and others reduces defensiveness, promotes open communication and encourages others to engage actively and contribute their best ideas.

CONFIDENCE BLOCKER: FEAR OF FAILURE

For many leaders, a significant barrier to Confidence is the fear of making mistakes. You might worry that an error will damage your credibility, reduce trust or invite criticism. This fear can lead to overly cautious decisions or reluctance to try new approaches, limiting both your personal growth and your team's potential. But Confidence isn't about perfection—it's about persistence and adaptability.

Entrepreneur, best-selling author and renowned thought leader Marie Forleo—known for her transformative work in personal development and business coaching—offers a mantra that perfectly captures the essence of Confidence: "Everything is Figureoutable" (also the title of her best-selling book)[18]. When you believe in your ability to figure things out, you can show up in a way that helps you overcome the fear of failure or getting it wrong.

One powerful way to shift from perfectionism to Confidence is by reframing failure as feedback. Viewing mistakes as opportunities for learning and growth allows you to model resilience for yourself and your team. To ease the fear of failure, try setting aside time for project post-mortems. These discussions—focusing on what worked, what didn't and what was learned—normalize setbacks as part of the process. This reinforces that Confidence isn't about always being right but about always being willing to learn.

CONFIDENCE IN ACTION

Meet Sarah. Sarah is a tech startup founder who led her team through a high-stakes product launch. Despite unexpected technical setbacks, she remained calm and transparent, openly sharing her thought process and inviting her team's input. By focusing on solutions rather than trying to appear unflappable, Sarah modeled a growth mindset that encouraged her team to tackle issues creatively. Her approach led to a successful launch and instilled a culture of resilience and trust that empowers her team for future challenges.

Sarah's Confidence came not from knowing every answer but from trusting that, together, they had the resources and skills to overcome any obstacle.

Sarah's approach extends beyond work into her role as a parent. When her child faces a new or daunting experience—like starting a new class or trying out for a sports team—Sarah expresses belief in their abilities and reinforces the value of effort and learning. She reassures them that mistakes are part of the process and emphasizes perseverance over perfection. By showing Confidence in her child's ability to grow, she helps build their resilience and self-trust.

SARAH'S CONFIDENCE GAME PLAN

Be transparent. In high-pressure situations, share thought processes openly to show that Confidence isn't about having all the answers but about tackling challenges together.

Value outside input. Invite team perspectives to foster trust, strengthen morale and empower collective problem-solving.

Focus on forward progress. Emphasize persistence over perfection by treating mistakes as learning opportunities, building Confidence through perseverance and adaptability.

HAPPINESS HUDDLE ☺

In what areas of your life could you model Confidence by focusing more on growth rather than perfection? How might this encourage those around you to take more risks and embrace learning?

DYNAMIC DUOS

In the playbook of happiness, some pillars are natural teammates, working together to amplify their impact. Confidence and Curiosity, for example, form a powerful duo in leadership and life. Confident people trust their abilities and embrace Curiosity, knowing they can handle whatever challenges arise. This pairing fosters innovative problem-solving, encourages feedback and supports calculated risks.

Confidence and Authenticity form another dynamic duo, strengthening trust and connection. Confidence gives leaders the assurance to show up as their true selves, while Authenticity reinforces the genuine relationships that build loyalty and collaboration. Together, they create a culture where people feel seen, valued and motivated to contribute at their best.

DYNAMIC DUO	HOW THEY WORK TOGETHER	IMPACT
Confidence + Curiosity	Confident leaders trust themselves enough to explore, ask questions and take risks.	Fosters innovative problem-solving and builds trust through openness and adaptability.
Confidence + Authenticity	Confidence empowers leaders to show up as their true selves, while Authenticity builds genuine connections.	Strengthens trust, loyalty and collaboration, creating a culture of engagement and inclusion.

When you practice Confidence in everyday situations, you strengthen your own self-trust and inspire those around you.

THE EIGHT PILLARS OF HAPPINESS

Leading with Confidence creates a culture of trust, encourages calculated risk-taking and supports an environment where people feel empowered to contribute fully.

I believe in you!

Here are some simple ways to inspire Confidence at work.

◇ **Celebrate small wins.** Recognize and celebrate small accomplishments in yourself and your team. Even small successes reinforce the sense that progress is being made and that challenges are surmountable.

◇ **Share your learning process.** When you encounter a challenge, share how you're tackling it with your team. Rather than presenting a perfect front, model how you learn and adapt through each step. This transparency normalizes learning and shows that Confidence doesn't require always having the answer—it's about trusting in your ability to find it.

Remember, like any skill, Confidence isn't built overnight. It strengthens through consistent, small acts of trust in yourself and those around you.

And now that we've explored Confidence, let's dive into the next pillar—Authenticity.

AUTHENTICITY

In a world full of expectations and ideals, we're often sold models of who we're "supposed" to be. Whether it's societal norms, workplace standards or external pressures, these expectations can make it hard to show up as our true selves. But when we try to fit into someone else's standards, we lose the connection to our own values and make it nearly impossible to live—or lead—with Authenticity.

Authenticity is about being true to yourself and aligning your actions with your values.

Authenticity is about being true to yourself and aligning your actions with your values. It's about rejecting external molds and embracing who you genuinely are. When you lead with Authenticity, you build trust, foster deeper connections and create an environment where others feel safe to do the same.

By bringing your whole self to work and life, you invite openness, acceptance and collaboration, paving the way for stronger relationships and more meaningful impact.

AUTHENTICITY QUICK FACTS

Builds trust and cohesion. People who live authentically experience higher levels of satisfaction and resilience. In leadership, Authenticity strengthens team trust and psychological safety.

Encourages open communication. Authenticity fosters environments where people feel safe to share ideas, voice concerns and engage deeply with their work.

Strengthens resilience. By staying true to your values, you reduce the stress of conformity and build the resilience needed to navigate challenges.

Drives innovation. When people feel safe to be themselves, they're more likely to contribute creative ideas and collaborate effectively.

AUTHENTICITY BLOCKER: THE PRESSURE TO CONFORM

For many leaders, a common challenge to Authenticity is the pressure to conform. High-stakes situations or diverse settings can create a disconnect between personal values and external expectations, making it difficult to show up authentically. This tension not only reduces effectiveness but can also erode trust over time.

To overcome this, start with small, genuine actions. Practice expressing your perspective openly and with empathy. Share a personal story during a meeting or acknowledge an area where you're still learning. These small, honest moments build trust and signal to others that it's safe to be genuine.

AUTHENTICITY IN ACTION

Meet Maria. Maria is an executive in a healthcare organization known for her openness and commitment to transparency. When her team faced an unexpected challenge—a delayed rollout of a major initiative—Maria gathered her team for an open discussion. Instead of assigning blame or hiding the difficulties, she shared the obstacles the team was facing, acknowledged her own frustrations and invited her team to collaborate on solutions. Her honesty inspired trust, encouraged creativity and brought the project back on track.

Maria's Authenticity extends beyond work. At home, she embraces her vulnerabilities and shares her challenges with her children, fostering mutual trust and respect. This openness strengthens her family bonds and makes her a more grounded and relatable leader at work.

MARIA'S AUTHENTICITY GAME PLAN

Foster transparency. Share both successes and setbacks openly to create a safe space for honest communication.

Encourage vulnerability. Acknowledge when you don't have all the answers to show that learning is valued over perfection.

Practice consistency. Align your values across work and home life to reinforce Authenticity in every area of your leadership.

HAPPINESS HUDDLE 😊

In what areas of your life do you feel most authentic? How could you bring more of that openness into your leadership?

DYNAMIC DUOS

Authenticity works alongside other happiness pillars to amplify its impact.

DYNAMIC DUO	HOW THEY WORK TOGETHER	IMPACT
Authenticity + Compassion	Authenticity fosters openness, while Compassion creates understanding and mutual respect.	Builds deep trust and collaboration, creating a foundation of psychological safety.
Authenticity + Confidence	Confidence empowers leaders to embrace their strengths, while Authenticity ensures they lead with honesty.	Strengthens team loyalty and engagement by modeling genuine, values-driven leadership.

Authenticity is about living your values and embracing vulnerability. While it requires courage to show up as your true self, the payoff is profound. Living authentically brings a sense of internal peace, as your actions align with your core values and your relationships become more meaningful. By consistently modeling honesty and openness, you inspire trust, foster collaboration and create a foundation of loyalty that drives both happiness and success.

Here are some simple ways to embrace Authenticity at work.

◇ **Make space for honest check-ins**. Set aside time during meetings or one-on-ones for genuine conversations. Sharing personal updates and inviting others to do the same creates a supportive, open environment.

◇ **Reflect on your core values**. Regularly take time to consider how your actions align with your principles. This practice keeps you grounded and ensures your leadership stays true to your values.

When you live and lead from a place of Authenticity, you create stronger, more genuine connections with those around you. Authenticity builds the trust and openness that make relationships richer and more resilient, while aligning your actions with your values creates a meaningful sense of purpose in all areas of your life.

Let's shift our focus to Purpose. While Authenticity centers on who you are and what you value, Purpose asks a different question—what drives you? It's about the deeper "why" behind your work and life and how aligning with it can inspire fulfillment and impact.

PURPOSE

Purpose is about having a sense of meaning and direction. It doesn't have to be big or profound—it simply needs to provide enough clarity to guide you forward and fuel your motivation. As Simon Sinek famously highlights in *Start with Why*, Purpose provides the clarity to move forward with confidence and focus[19].

> **Purpose is about having a sense of meaning and direction.**

Your "why" doesn't have to be grand to be meaningful. It can be as simple as committing to helping others grow, creating an inclusive work environment or fostering a supportive family. Purpose gives you a steady anchor, helping you navigate change and ensuring your actions align with what matters most *to you*.

When you lead with Purpose, you create a sense of alignment that inspires you and motivates those around you to contribute to a shared vision. It's what allows you to stay grounded in change, focus your energy on meaningful actions and drive engagement and impact in your life and work.

PURPOSE QUICK FACTS

◇ **Inspires engagement and motivation.** Research shows that people with a clear sense of Purpose experience greater happiness.

◇ **Boosts team alignment.** Purpose-driven leadership fosters unity by helping team members see how their work contributes to larger goals.

◇ **Supports resilience.** A strong sense of Purpose provides stability during uncertainty, helping individuals and teams navigate challenges with confidence.

◇ **Strengthens loyalty and trust.** Purpose gives people a reason to stay committed, fostering a sense of belonging and shared meaning within organizations.

PURPOSE BLOCKER: THE PRESSURE TO PRIORITIZE RESULTS

One of the biggest obstacles to Purpose is the relentless pressure to prioritize results. Traditional management models often measure success through efficiency, deadlines and immediate outcomes. Leaders are frequently pulled into this cycle, where short-term wins are valued over long-term impact. While this approach can drive productivity temporarily, it often leaves leaders and their teams feeling burnt out, disconnected and unsure of the bigger picture.

It's easy to feel trapped in this mindset, especially in fast-paced environments where the stakes are high. You may find yourself questioning whether there's time to think about Purpose when every moment seems accounted for. But focusing solely on results often sacrifices the deeper meaning and motivation that make leadership truly effective.

To break free from this trap, it's essential to anchor Purpose in your daily actions. Small, intentional choices—like setting an intention each morning or aligning routine tasks with your values—can help you reconnect with the "why" behind your work. These moments reinforce that productivity and Purpose can coexist and that meaningful progress often starts with simple, thoughtful steps.

PURPOSE IN ACTION

Meet Clara. Clara leads an educational nonprofit with a mission to make quality education accessible to all. Her deep sense of Purpose drives everything she does, from guiding her team to navigating challenges. Clara frequently reminds her team of the impact their work has on students and communities, sharing success stories that create a strong emotional connection to their mission.

When faced with budget cuts, Clara rallied her team to find creative solutions that kept essential programs running. Her unwavering commitment to Purpose empowered her team to stay motivated and resilient during difficult times.

Clara's dedication extends beyond work. She volunteers at a community center, using her skills to support under-resourced schools. For Clara, Purpose isn't about grand gestures—it's about aligning her daily actions with her values. Her approach inspires her team and family to find their own sense of Purpose, fostering meaning and fulfillment

---

CLARA'S PURPOSE GAME PLAN

Reinforce Purpose in team interactions. Regularly remind your team of the impact their work has on the organization's mission or community.

Celebrate small wins. Acknowledge how individual contributions support shared goals, boosting morale and fostering a sense of unity.

Model Purpose in your personal life. Align your actions outside of work with your core values to show that Purpose is a consistent, guiding principle.

HAPPINESS HUDDLE ☺

What drives you to show up every day? Reflect on one way you could integrate more Purpose into your daily routine, either at work or in your personal life.

DYNAMIC DUOS

Purpose works alongside other happiness pillars to create meaningful engagement.

DYNAMIC DUO	HOW THEY WORK TOGETHER	IMPACT
Purpose + Authenticity	Purpose gives you direction, while Authenticity ensures your actions align with your values.	Builds integrity, trust and a sense of shared mission.
Purpose + Compassion	Purpose fosters a shared mission, while Compassion ensures the needs of others are considered.	Creates a collaborative culture where people feel valued and motivated.

Integrating Purpose into your life doesn't require sweeping changes. Intentional action can deepen your connection to what matters most.

Here are two simple practices to embrace Purpose.

◇ **Set an intention each morning.** Start your day with a specific goal that is aligned with your values—like supporting a colleague, being present or contributing creatively to a project.

◇ **Reflect on meaningful moments.** At the end of each day, recall one interaction or task that aligned with your Purpose. This practice reinforces the value of Purpose in your life and strengthens your commitment.

Purpose isn't reserved for grand missions—it's a mindset you can cultivate through consistent, everyday choices. By leading with Purpose, you align your actions with your values, deepen your connection to meaningful work and create lasting impact in your life and leadership. Purpose inspires motivation, fosters collaboration and strengthens resilience, helping to build a culture where everyone feels connected to shared goals.

Purpose guides us toward what's meaningful while helping us navigate the challenges of leadership. Now we'll explore the pillar of Compassion and how it enriches both leadership and life.

COMPASSION

Compassion means showing kindness and grace to yourself and others. It's about seeing and valuing the humanity in those around you and taking intentional action to support them. In leadership, Compassion creates an environment where people feel safe bringing their full selves to work, knowing they're valued far beyond their productivity.

> # Compassion means showing kindness and grace to yourself and others.

Right now the world needs Compassion more than ever. And as leaders, we have a responsibility to show up with empathy, understanding and care—not just for the people we work with but for the broader communities and systems we're all part of. Knowing how energy works from the Energy-Impact Model, we understand that our choices and actions radiate outward in ways that go far beyond us. The decisions we make on our side of the world influence and shape outcomes on the other.

Compassion is a skill that allows us to lead with this interconnectedness in mind. It challenges us to consider the full range of our shared humanity and to lead in ways that prioritize care, equity and inclusion. Compassionate leadership is about recognizing the profound impact of our energy and making choices that contribute to collective flourishing and growth.

When leaders practice Compassion, they reduce stress, build trust and strengthen connections. Compassion creates the psychological safety needed for collaboration, innovation and shared success. By leading with Compassion, we not only support our teams but we model the kind of leadership that inspires meaningful change in the world.

COMPASSION QUICK FACTS

◇ **Reduces stress.** Compassion lowers stress levels, improving mental clarity and focus for both leaders and teams.

◇ **Boosts engagement.** Employees who feel valued and supported are more motivated and loyal, leading to higher engagement and retention.

◇ **Strengthens resilience.** Compassionate leadership fosters trust and psychological safety, helping teams navigate challenges with confidence.

◇ **Drives performance.** Compassion reduces defensiveness and creates an open environment where people feel safe to collaborate and innovate.

COMPASSION BLOCKER: THE FEAR OF APPEARING WEAK

One common obstacle to Compassion is the fear of being perceived as weak or too soft. Traditional management models often prioritize authority and efficiency, leading leaders to believe they must avoid showing vulnerability or personal connection. This approach, as we've seen, can result in detachment, a lack of trust and diminished morale.

Compassionate leadership is about guiding with both empathy and accountability. We can—and need to—reframe Compassion as a strength.

Because it is. It offers a balanced approach that prioritizes people while maintaining high expectations. By fully listening to your team members' needs and communicating clear goals, you create an environment of mutual respect and accountability. This balanced approach demonstrates that Compassion is a leadership asset, not a liability.

THE POWER OF SELF-COMPASSION

Self-compassion means showing yourself the same kindness and understanding you'd offer a friend. It's especially important during setbacks or moments of fear. Research shows that self-compassion reduces self-criticism, amplifies resilience and helps you stay grounded in tough times.[20]

When leaders practice self-compassion, they model it for their teams, fostering a culture of psychological safety where mistakes are seen as learning opportunities. This approach encourages innovation, reduces fear of failure[21] and supports a growth mindset. Beyond work, self-compassion deepens patience and empathy in all relationships, helping you lead with both vulnerability and strength[22].

ACTION SHOT ☆

When self-doubt creeps in, pause and ask, *How would I support a team member in this situation?* Then, show yourself the same compassion.

COMPASSION IN ACTION

Meet Maya. Maya is a director at a nonprofit known for her warmth and ability to connect with her team. When a team member, Tom, faced personal challenges affecting his work, Maya approached him privately to understand his situation better. Instead of jumping to conclusions, she listened to his concerns and helped him explore solutions that balanced his workload with his well-being.

This conversation not only helped Tom regain his balance but also reinforced trust within the team. Maya's Compassion allowed Tom to feel supported, re-engage with his work and ultimately improve his performance. Her approach set a powerful example for her team, fostering a culture of trust and openness.

At home, Maya's Compassion extends to her role as a parent. She listens actively to her children's worries, encouraging open discussions and modeling empathy. This consistency in her leadership—both at work and at home—amplifies understanding and support in every area of her life.

MAYA'S COMPASSION GAME PLAN

Be present. Set aside distractions and give full attention to team members, showing that their challenges and perspectives matter.

Offer support with accountability. Balance empathy with clear expectations, helping others navigate challenges while staying focused on shared goals.

Model Compassion for others. Leading with empathy reinforces a culture where Compassion is a shared value that drives connection and growth.

HAPPINESS HUDDLE ☺

How can you practice Compassion in your daily leadership? Consider one way you could show empathy or support to a team member today.

DYNAMIC DUOS

Compassion amplifies other happiness pillars by fostering trust and openness.

DYNAMIC DUO	HOW THEY WORK TOGETHER	IMPACT
Compassion + Authenticity	Authenticity allows leaders to connect genuinely, while Compassion ensures those connections are rooted in kindness and grace.	Builds deeper trust and psychological safety, fostering a culture of respect and collaboration.
Compassion + Gratitude	Compassion supports people's needs, while Gratitude highlights and celebrates their contributions.	Strengthens relationships and boosts morale, creating a positive and motivated team culture.

Cultivating Compassion doesn't require grand gestures. Small acts of kindness and support can have a powerful impact.

Here are two simple practices to help you lead with Compassion.

◇ **Begin meetings with a personal check-in.** Ask team members how they're doing, showing genuine interest in their well-being. This small step fosters a supportive environment and sets the tone for open communication.

◇ **Practice active encouragement.** Make a conscious effort to recognize team members' strengths and acknowledge their efforts, especially during challenging times. Encouragement reinforces trust and helps people feel valued.

By consistently leading with kindness and grace, you create a foundation of support, trust and connection that empowers your team to do the same—for themselves and one another.

Compassion strengthens the bonds that keep teams connected, but it also works in harmony with another vital pillar: Gratitude. Let's explore how cultivating appreciation can deepen relationships, fuel resilience and enrich both your leadership and your life.

GRATITUDE

Gratitude is perhaps the most well-known and widely accepted of the happiness pillars. Gratitude journals are a celebrated habit and some companies even gift them to employees as a way to encourage appreciation. But as with all the Eight Pillars, knowing Gratitude's importance on a personal level doesn't mean we're designing for it on a communal level.

Gratitude is the intentional act of recognizing and appreciating the positive aspects of life. In leadership, it goes beyond simply saying thank you. Practicing Gratitude means consistently acknowledging the contributions, progress and efforts of those around you. By leading with Gratitude, you foster a culture of appreciation, recognition and mutual support, creating a team dynamic where everyone is motivated to bring their best.

Gratitude is the intentional act of recognizing and appreciating the positive aspects of life.

Gratitude doesn't just boost morale—it strengthens resilience, focus and collaboration. Research shows that when team members feel appreciated, they're more engaged, creative and willing to go the extra mile[23]. And during high-pressure periods, Gratitude becomes a stabilizing force, helping teams stay grounded and resilient.

And that's the key—while The Eight Pillars are all about creating positive energy to fuel engagement and impact, the broader we design for practicing them, the better off we all are. Gratitude has to be accepted as more than a personal practice. It needs to be seen as a powerful tool for strengthening relationships and building a culture where everyone feels connected and empowered to contribute.

GRATITUDE QUICK FACTS

◇ **Boosts mental health.** Gratitude improves happiness and reduces stress by activating the brain's reward system.

◇ **Fosters team cohesion.** Teams that practice Gratitude experience stronger connections, greater trust and more collaboration.

◇ **Improves retention.** Employees who feel valued are more likely to stay loyal to their teams and organizations.

◇ **Increases productivity.** Grateful leaders and team members approach tasks with greater positivity and focus, leading to higher-quality outcomes.

GRATITUDE BLOCKER: THE TENDENCY TO FOCUS ON PROBLEMS

As humans, we're hardwired with a negativity bias—a survival mechanism that makes us more likely to notice problems, potential threats and negative outcomes. While this served our ancestors well in avoiding danger, it can create challenges in modern leadership. The instinct to zero in on what's not working often leads us to focus on problems and overlook wins, progress and contributions.

In fast-paced environments, this bias is amplified by the pressure to solve issues quickly. While addressing challenges is essential, an unbalanced focus on problems can reduce morale, leaving achievements unrecognized and team efforts undervalued.

Gratitude is your tool to counteract negativity bias and rewire your brain to see possibility and goodness. By intentionally recognizing the positive aspects of your work, team and daily experiences, you can shift your mindset and create a more balanced perspective. Start by reflecting on specific moments of Gratitude, whether it's celebrating a recent success, appreciating someone's extra effort or valuing the support you received during a tough moment.

Encourage your team to embrace Gratitude, too. Incorporate moments of appreciation into meetings or casual conversations. This small but intentional shift rewires how you and your team perceive challenges and opportunities, fostering a positive, energized atmosphere where contributions are valued and motivation thrives.

GRATITUDE IN ACTION

Meet Michael. Michael is a manager at a large warehouse facility who has made Gratitude a cornerstone of his leadership style. Each month, he hosts "Bright Spots"—short team huddles where employees share recent accomplishments and recognize one another's contributions. Michael highlights both major achievements—like meeting shipping deadlines during peak seasons—and everyday efforts, such as a team member stepping up to cover a shift or assisting a coworker with a heavy workload.

These meetings have transformed the team's culture. Over time, employees began thanking one another more frequently, creating an atmosphere of mutual appreciation and trust. This focus on Gratitude not only boosts day-to-day morale but also strengthens resilience during high-pressure times, like inventory audits or holiday rushes.

Michael's commitment to Gratitude extends beyond the workplace. He writes thank-you notes to colleagues, friends and even vendors, celebrating their unique contributions to the facility's success. This consistent practice of showing appreciation fosters stronger connections and motivates his team, creating a sense of shared purpose that sustains them through any challenge.

MICHAEL'S GRATITUDE GAME PLAN

Celebrate wins–both big and small. Recognize milestones and everyday contributions, showing that all efforts are valued and essential to the team's success.

Encourage team appreciation. Create opportunities for others to practice Gratitude and thank one another, reinforcing trust and connection.

Show Gratitude consistently. Make appreciation a regular part of leadership, building a culture where everyone feels valued and motivated to perform at their best.

HAPPINESS HUDDLE ☺

How can you incorporate Gratitude into your leadership and daily routine? Consider one way you could recognize your team's efforts this week, and observe the impact it has on their motivation and connection.

DYNAMIC DUOS

Gratitude works in harmony with other happiness pillars to amplify positivity and resilience.

DYNAMIC DUO	HOW THEY WORK TOGETHER	IMPACT
Gratitude + Compassion	Gratitude fosters appreciation for others, while Compassion ensures those connections are rooted in kindness and care.	Creates an empathetic, trusting culture where individuals feel valued and supported.
Gratitude + Optimism	Gratitude highlights the positive, reinforcing Optimism's focus on possibility and opportunity.	Builds a culture of hope, resilience and collective progress, even during challenges.

Like the other pillars, Gratitude doesn't require grand gestures. Instead, consistent acts of appreciation can create a lasting impact, deepening relationships and building a positive, resilient team culture.

Here are two ways to nurture Gratitude at work.

⬦ **End the day with a Gratitude reflection.** Take a few minutes at the end of each day to reflect on one or two things you're grateful for, like a work achievement, a meaningful conversation or a small moment of joy.

⬦ **Write a thank-you note each week.** Choose a team member, colleague or friend and send a short, specific note of appreciation. This simple act strengthens connections and lets people know their efforts are valued.

For leaders, Gratitude isn't just about recognition—it's part of a broader vision that values each team member's role in achieving shared goals. Embracing Gratitude allows you to foster an inclusive environment where everyone feels valued and motivated.

Gratitude fosters connection and appreciation, but it also opens the door to Curiosity. Let's explore how Curiosity fuels growth, innovation and deeper understanding in leadership and life.

CURIOSITY

I'll admit it—Curiosity might be my favorite of The Eight Pillars. Maybe it's because it comes so naturally to me, or maybe it's because the world needs so much more of it. We need more awe and wonder. We need to dream more, ask different questions and allow ourselves to imagine new possibilities. Curiosity invites us to see the world not just as it is but as it could be, and in doing so, it fuels the positive energy that drives growth and innovation.

> **Curiosity is the desire to seek out new experiences and learning opportunities.**

Curiosity is the desire to seek out new experiences and learning opportunities, with the belief that doing so broadens understanding and fuels growth—for yourself and those around you. It's not just about asking questions–it's a mindset of openness that drives exploration and discovery.

In leadership, Curiosity is transformative. It means intentionally creating a culture where questions, ideas and fresh perspectives are welcome. A curious leader models this approach, encouraging their team to think differently, explore new approaches and bring bold ideas forward. In a world of rapid change, a culture of Curiosity keeps your team adaptable, engaged and connected.

CURIOSITY QUICK FACTS

⬦ **Increases life satisfaction.** Research by Dr. Todd Kashdan shows that cultivating Curiosity increases satisfaction and well-being[24].

⬦ **Activates the brain's reward system.** Curiosity releases dopamine, improving mood and increasing motivation.

⬦ **Enhances adaptability.** People who embrace Curiosity handle challenges with resilience and a positive outlook.

⬦ **Fuels innovation.** Curious teams generate more creative solutions and approach problems with openness and collaboration.

CURIOSITY BLOCKER: THE FEAR OF LOOKING UNINFORMED

Let's face it—being curious can sometimes feel risky. In environments where expertise is highly valued, asking questions or seeking help may seem like a sign of weakness. This fear can cause both leaders and team members alike to avoid exploring new ideas or admitting when they don't know something, sticking instead to familiar processes.

But Curiosity isn't about knowing everything—it's about learning what you can. When you reframe Curiosity as a strength that drives growth, you remove the pressure to always have the answers. Start by modeling Curiosity openly in your own leadership. Share what you're learning or exploring and show your team that questions are tools for innovation, not a sign of incompetence.

When team members see that Curiosity is valued over ego, they feel safer to ask questions, admit gaps in knowledge and explore new possibilities. This creates a culture where learning is celebrated and collaboration thrives.

CURIOSITY IN ACTION

Meet Rachel. Rachel leads a fast-growing creative agency where Curiosity is at the heart of everything her team does. She regularly hosts "What if?" sessions, encouraging her team to brainstorm bold ideas without fear of judgment. She kicks things off with open-ended questions like, *What if we approached this from a completely different angle?* or *How could we turn this challenge into an opportunity?*

Rachel creates a safe, engaging environment by celebrating every contribution, no matter how unconventional. She'll ask follow-up questions like, *How could we bring that to life?* or *What might this idea look like if we expanded it?* This openness signals that Curiosity and exploration are essential to the team's success.

Over time, Rachel's team has developed a reputation for delivering standout campaigns. For example, a junior designer once shared a rough idea she'd been hesitant to voice. Rachel's encouragement turned that idea into an award-winning campaign, boosting both the project's success and the designer's confidence.

Rachel's Curiosity doesn't just drive creative breakthroughs—it builds a culture where every team member feels empowered to explore and contribute. By modeling Curiosity as a core value, she inspires her team to prioritize growth and collaboration, creating a workplace where innovation thrives.

RACHEL'S CURIOSITY GAME PLAN

Host "What if?" sessions. Dedicate regular time for brainstorming bold, untested ideas in a judgment-free zone.

Ask follow-up questions. Show genuine interest in every idea by asking questions that validate and expand on contributions.

Celebrate learning. Make space for team reflections, like discussing what they learned each week or tackling problems with fresh perspectives.

HAPPINESS HUDDLE ☺

How can you create space for Curiosity in your team? Think of one way you could encourage open exploration or make it safer for team members to share bold, untested ideas.

DYNAMIC DUOS

Curiosity works powerfully alongside other happiness pillars to create a culture of openness and innovation.

DYNAMIC DUO	HOW THEY WORK TOGETHER	IMPACT
Curiosity + Confidence	Confident leaders embrace Curiosity, trusting their ability to explore new ideas and navigate uncertainty.	Encourages innovative thinking and strengthens resilience in the face of challenges.

DYNAMIC DUO	HOW THEY WORK TOGETHER	IMPACT
Curiosity + Compassion	Curiosity fosters understanding, while Compassion ensures leaders approach others with empathy and care.	Builds trust, respect and deeper connections within the team.

Practicing Curiosity means staying open to wonder, awe and possibility. It's about creating space for exploration in your day, deepening your connections, fostering adaptability and inviting more happiness into your life.

Here are two simple practices to help you nurture Curiosity.

◇ **Ask "What surprised you today?"** This simple question shifts focus from routine to discovery, fostering awareness and openness. Use it as a journaling prompt, a team check-in or a family conversation starter.

◇ **Try "Yes, and…" conversations.** Borrowed from the world of improv, this practice builds on ideas instead of shutting them down, encouraging creativity and exploration.

Curiosity opens a door to a world of possibilities. It transforms routine interactions into opportunities for growth, and sparks connections that go beyond surface-level exchanges. By embracing each experience with a mindset of wonder, you fuel personal and organizational growth, setting the stage for innovation, collaboration and joy.

Curiosity invites us to dream of what could be and Optimism gives us the courage to believe it's possible. Let's explore how a positive outlook can elevate your leadership and inspire your team.

OPTIMISM

Optimism means focusing on positive outcomes and possibilities. It's about seeing potential and possibilities, even when the path ahead is uncertain. As a leader, this doesn't mean ignoring challenges or glossing over difficulties with toxic positivity—both can undermine trust and harm team culture. Instead, Optimism invites you to balance reality with hope, focusing on constructive solutions and keeping your team motivated toward shared goals.

Optimism means focusing on positive outcomes and possibilities.

Optimistic leaders look for opportunities within obstacles, trusting in their team's ability to overcome setbacks. They don't dismiss the hard stuff–they acknowledge it while maintaining a forward-focused perspective that inspires creativity. When you lead with Optimism, you create an environment where challenges are seen as opportunities for growth.

Optimism energizes results. Teams led by optimistic leaders tend to pursue creative solutions, recover more quickly from setbacks and maintain higher levels of engagement. During high-pressure periods, Optimism becomes a stabilizing force, helping teams stay grounded, motivated and focused. It fuels resilience and adaptability while reinforcing a culture of trust and collaboration.

OPTIMISM QUICK FACTS

✧ **Boosts resilience.** Optimism helps manage stress and sustain focus through challenges.

✧ **Enhances creativity and motivation.** Optimism fuels innovation and problem-solving.

✧ **Strengthens trust.** Optimistic leaders create psychological safety, encouraging collaboration and bold ideas.

✧ **Promotes adaptability.** Optimistic teams view setbacks as opportunities, driving growth and improvement.

OPTIMISM BLOCKER: FEAR OF APPEARING UNREALISTIC

A common obstacle to practicing Optimism is the fear of being perceived as naïve or out of touch. Some leaders worry that focusing on possibilities might overshadow challenges or make them seem unrealistic. However, Optimism isn't about ignoring problems—it's about acknowledging them while maintaining a belief in forward momentum.

Reframe Optimism as a balanced approach. Realistic Optimism allows you to validate your team's concerns while also providing hope and a path forward. By focusing on achievable goals and celebrating small wins, you create an environment that prioritizes both progress and positivity. This approach reassures your team that Optimism is grounded in action, not blind faith.

OPTIMISM IN ACTION

Meet Janet, a director at a regional bank navigating significant shifts in the financial market. Faced with declining interest rates and increased competition, Janet encouraged her team to reimagine their strategies. Rather than focusing solely on the challenges, she reframed the situation as an opportunity to innovate. She prompted her team to explore creative solutions, such as offering personalized financial products and strengthening local partnerships to differentiate their services.

Janet kept morale high by consistently emphasizing their shared mission of serving the community and celebrating small successes, like landing new partnerships or improving client satisfaction scores. Her balanced Optimism—acknowledging the challenges while focusing on actionable solutions—kept her team motivated and engaged. Together, they not only adapted but positioned the bank for long-term growth and strengthened their reputation in the region.

Janet's leadership highlights how Optimism fuels resilience and creativity. By maintaining a forward-looking perspective, she inspired her team to approach obstacles as opportunities, fostering confidence and a culture of innovation.

JANET'S OPTIMISM GAME PLAN

Reframe limitations as opportunities. Encourage others to explore new perspectives and strategies that emerge from the current situation.

Emphasize shared purpose. Remind people the value of their work to keep them aligned and motivated.

Celebrate progress. Highlight achievements along the way to sustain momentum and morale.

HAPPINESS HUDDLE 😊

In what areas of your life or leadership could you cultivate more Optimism and how might this shift your outlook and impact those around you? Reflect on how a more optimistic approach could strengthen resilience, morale and success across your team.

THE PROJECT: MORE HAPPY PODCAST

The Project: More Happy Podcast is one of my favorite ways to practice Optimism. Through conversations with visionaries from all walks of life, we explore hopeful, actionable visions for a future that's more just, sustainable and deeply rooted in our shared humanity.

Listening to these diverse voices isn't just inspiring—it's a reminder of what's possible when we focus on solutions and collective impact. Each episode invites listeners to imagine and create a world designed for happiness and human flourishing, reinforcing that Optimism is about more than hope—it's about action.

Listen wherever you stream your favorite podcasts.

DYNAMIC DUOS

Optimism works powerfully alongside other happiness pillars to build resilience and foster a forward-focused, supportive culture.

DYNAMIC DUO	HOW THEY WORK TOGETHER	IMPACT
Optimism + Gratitude	Gratitude helps leaders focus on and celebrate positive aspects of work, enhancing their natural Optimism.	Fosters a culture of appreciation and positivity, reinforcing team resilience and morale.
Optimism + Confidence	Confidence empowers leaders to tackle challenges with courage, while Optimism keeps the focus on possibilities.	Strengthens resilience and creates actionable optimism, turning setbacks into opportunities.

Practicing Optimism means focusing on what's possible, even in the face of challenges. It's about shifting your perspective to see opportunities, fostering resilience and energizing your team to move forward with purpose.

Here are two simple practices to help you nurture Optimism.

⬦ **Focus on what's working.** Take time each week to identify successes—big or small—for yourself and your team. Shifting attention from problems to progress fosters a constructive mindset and builds momentum.

⬦ **Set daily intentions.** Start each day by setting an intention aligned with your long-term goals. This practice creates a positive frame for your day, keeping you motivated and grounded in possibility.

Optimism isn't just about looking on the bright side. It's a skill rooted in actionable hope and a forward-focused mindset. By practicing Optimism, you inspire creativity and create an environment fueled by forward momentum.

Optimism gives us the strength to envision what's possible, while Feeling ensures our leadership is rooted in emotional awareness. Let's explore how tuning into emotions deepens connections and strengthens every aspect of leadership.

FEELING

Feeling means being attuned to and expressing emotions in healthy ways. It's about recognizing and managing emotions constructively—for yourself and for those around you. Emotions aren't problems to avoid— they're valuable messengers that guide us toward deeper understanding and connection.

> **Feeling means being attuned to and expressing emotions in healthy ways.**

Yet whenever I teach The Eight Pillars of Happiness, this is the pillar people resist most. The emotional reaction to Feeling is often discomfort or even disgust—but deep down, it's fear. We're afraid to tune into our feelings for fear of what we might uncover.

But Feeling is a strength, not a weakness. And emotional intelligence— the ability to understand and work with emotions—is critical for building the sense of belonging that every human craves. When we embrace Feeling, we are better able to connect with one another, build trust and have meaningful relationships. And as we grow more comfortable with our emotions, we create environments where others feel safe to do the same.

There's another misconception we need to clear up. Despite what we've been told all our lives, the opposite of happiness isn't sadness. Sadness exists on the same spectrum as happiness—they're teammates, not adversaries. Happiness is an action. And the opposite of action is inaction. The real opposite of happiness is complacency. When we're complacent, we stagnate. We stop taking initiative to create more happiness in our lives or the world.

Okay, back to the happiness pillar of Feeling. When you embrace Feeling as a leader, you unlock a powerful tool for building trust and connection. Emotional awareness helps you create spaces where others feel seen, valued and understood—laying the foundation for a workplace culture that thrives on mutual respect and collaboration.

FEELING QUICK FACTS

◇ **Builds connection.** Emotional awareness fosters environments where people feel safe to express themselves, strengthening bonds and driving collaboration.

◇ **Boosts resilience.** Leaders who understand and manage emotions constructively inspire teams to approach challenges calmly and with greater focus.

◇ **Enhances team cohesion.** Emotional awareness supports honest communication, which helps teams stay aligned, engaged and motivated to perform at their best.

◇ **Improves retention.** Employees who feel valued and emotionally safe are more likely to stay loyal to their organizations.

FEELING BLOCKER: THE STIGMA OF EMOTIONS AT WORK

Many leaders hesitate to embrace Feeling because they believe emotions don't belong in the workplace. They worry that acknowledging emotions might undermine their authority, blur professional boundaries or signal weakness. For women leaders, this fear is often amplified by societal double standards. Women who express emotions at work are frequently labeled as irrational, overly sensitive or unpredictable, while men exhibiting similar emotions are seen as passionate or strong. These biases discourage emotional authenticity, forcing women in particular to suppress their feelings to be taken seriously.

This avoidant approach harms more than just the person expressing their emotions—it increases misunderstandings, stress and conflict across teams, ultimately hurting morale and productivity.

It's really important that we reframe emotional awareness as a leadership strength. Emotions, when acknowledged and managed constructively, provide critical insight into team dynamics and individual motivations. Happy Leaders can start by modeling small moments of emotional openness. For example, share your experiences with honesty—*This was tough for me, but here's how I worked through it*—and invite your team to do the same. This transparency helps dismantle harmful stereotypes and reinforces that Feeling is not just acceptable—it's valuable for building trust, connection and authentic leadership.

FEELING IN ACTION

Meet Leah. Leah is an HR director at a regional tech company and she's on a mission to create a workplace where emotions are acknowledged and respected. When the company underwent a major restructuring, many employees felt anxious and uncertain. Leah knew she needed to address these emotions head-on.

She introduced optional Insight Circles where employees could share their challenges and successes in a supportive, nonjudgmental setting. These gatherings quickly became a cornerstone of the company's culture. Employees felt safe to express themselves, knowing their emotions would be heard and validated. Rather than venting sessions, these circles provided a space to process feelings, gain perspective and move toward meaningful action.

Leah's leadership not only helped her team navigate a stressful period—it strengthened their trust and resilience. Employees reported feeling more connected to one another and more motivated to contribute. Leah's focus on emotional openness created a ripple effect of engagement and loyalty, proving that Feeling is a powerful tool for growth.

LEAH'S FEELING GAME PLAN

Create spaces for connection. Establish regular forums where people can share challenges and wins openly and without judgment.

Model emotional openness. Be honest about experiences and emotions when appropriate to help normalize emotional expression for others.

Balance emotions with focus. Acknowledge feelings while remaining solution-oriented to demonstrate a constructive approach during tough times.

HAPPINESS HUDDLE ☺

How can you integrate emotional awareness into your leadership? Think of one small step you could take to create space for emotions within your team.

DYNAMIC DUOS

Feeling works with other happiness pillars to create trust and genuine connection.

DYNAMIC DUO	HOW THEY WORK TOGETHER	IMPACT
Feeling + Compassion	Feeling increases emotional awareness, while Compassion channels those emotions into care and understanding.	Builds an empathetic culture where team members feel supported, valued and safe to contribute.
Feeling + Authenticity	Feeling allows leaders to recognize their emotions, while Authenticity ensures they express them genuinely.	Strengthens trust and openness, creating an environment where respect and collaboration thrive.

Feeling requires consistency. Building emotional awareness into your routine doesn't demand major shifts, but it does require regular practice.

Here are two simple ways to nurture Feeling in your leadership and life.

⬦ **Pause to recognize emotions in the moment**. When you feel a strong emotion, take a brief pause to identify it and reflect on its impact. This strengthens self-awareness and helps you respond intentionally.

✧ **Host a pulse check on projects**. Ask your team to reflect on what energized them and what added stress during a recent project. Encourage open sharing to build understanding and identify ways to boost motivation.

Feeling is a leadership superpower. By valuing your own and others' emotions, you build a culture of trust and belonging. Emotional awareness strengthens relationships, fosters resilience and ensures that the environments you create are ones where people feel empowered to thrive.

THE EIGHT PILLARS OF HAPPINESS ARE YOUR GUIDE TO CREATING POSITIVE ENERGY.

As Maya Angelou so beautifully put it, happiness is about thriving with *"passion, compassion, humor, and style.[25]"* The Eight Pillars of Happiness make that possible. By practicing them, you're not just transforming your own life—you're equipping yourself with the tools to generate the energy that drives engagement and impact. As a leader, you have the power to intentionally create environments where happiness fuels momentum and purpose, setting the stage for meaningful outcomes.

Each pillar represents a learnable skill that amplifies your ability to lead. These let you build the energy you need to stay adaptable, creative and deeply connected. Curiosity and Compassion foster bold, inclusive problem-solving. Confidence and Authenticity deepen trust and make relationships more powerful. Gratitude and Optimism create the resilience and motivation to tackle challenges head-on. Feeling strengthens your emotional awareness, allowing you to lead with empathy and build genuine connections. Purpose aligns your actions with meaning, providing the clarity and drive to stay focused on what truly matters. All together these skills allow you to design a leadership style—and a life—that is grounded in the kind of energy that inspires action.

That is your superpower.

When you prioritize happiness as a leader, you're not only influencing your team but also their families, communities and the larger world. A team member who feels seen and supported at work goes home with greater energy, contributing to healthier relationships and a more fulfilled life. Over time, Happy Leaders create legacies of positive impact that transcend industries and generations.

Congratulations on completing this first step in your journey to mastering the science of happiness! By exploring The Eight Pillars of Happiness, you've built a foundation for creating the positive energy that fuels engagement and impact. Along the way, you've also learned how the Energy-Impact Model connects personal energy to team engagement and meaningful results. Together these two science-backed tools empower you to cultivate happiness as a skill, amplifying your ability to lead and positively influence everyone around you.

But this is just the beginning. In the next section I'll introduce you to a powerful leadership tool for boosting energy when you need it most—Power-Ups. Power-Ups help you generate more positive energy at home, at work and in your relationships. We'll explore how to take the models we've learned—the Energy-Impact Model and The Eight Pillars of Happiness—and put them to work when you need them most.

You now have the foundation. It's time to energize your leadership and design a life that inspires action and impact. Let's dive in.

#TLDR: KEY TAKEAWAYS

1. **Happiness requires action.** The Eight Pillars of Happiness—Confidence, Authenticity, Purpose, Compassion, Gratitude, Optimism, Curiosity and Feeling—are actionable skills that generate the energy needed for engagement and impact.

2. **The Eight Pillars work both individually and together.** Practicing any pillar strengthens your happiness, but combining them amplifies their power.

3. **The Eight Pillars fuel positive energy.** By practicing them, you generate the energy that increases engagement in yourself and your team, ultimately creating a foundation for meaningful and lasting impact in your work and life.

ACTION SHOT ☆

Choose one pillar to focus on this week. Practice it intentionally by setting a small goal or habit that supports this skill (e.g., for Gratitude, try listing three things you're grateful for each day).

HAPPINESS HUDDLE ☺

Which of the Eight Pillars comes naturally to you? Which one could you develop further to enhance your happiness and impact? Think about how focusing on this pillar could positively influence your life and work.

Part 2:
Lead for Impact

Use Power-Ups to align energy
and amplify impact in home,
work and in relationships.

CHAPTER 4

Using Power-Ups to Supercharge Energy

"Positivity is like a muscle. The more you use it, the stronger it gets."
— Arianna Huffington

Now that we know how happiness works—how positive energy leads to increased engagement and greater impact–and we understand the role of The Eight Pillars of Happiness, we have to start putting it into action to supercharge our team and life. We have to build more positive energy.

And just like building physical strength, building energy takes practice, repetition and intentional effort. You wouldn't hit the gym once and expect to run a marathon the next day, right? The same applies to cultivating happiness. It's about consistently showing up, putting in the work and celebrating the progress along the way.

Happy Leaders know this because they know that happiness is a skill. It's not something you wait for—it's something you create, refine and apply in the moments that matter. In the last chapter, we uncovered a game-changing truth–happiness can be intentionally created. And The Eight Pillars of Happiness are the roadmap for doing it. The pillars are practical skills that shape how you show up for yourself and others.

But even the most grounded Happy Leaders know there are moments when life demands more—when challenges feel overwhelming, focus starts to slip or impact needs a sharp boost. In those moments, having simple, intentional practices that re-energize you and your team can make all the difference.

That's where Power-Ups come in. Power-Ups are targeted, science-backed practices that boost engagement and impact. They are designed to supercharge your energy and focus exactly where and when you need it most. They go beyond practicing individual pillars, combining their strengths into focused practices that help you and your team rise to the occasion.

Happy Leaders use Power-Ups to stay energized and engaged. Whether it's navigating a difficult conversation, resetting after a tough day or reigniting creativity, Power-Ups are how you take what you've learned about happiness, energy and impact and apply it with precision and purpose.

Power-Ups are not a replacement for The Eight Pillars. They're an amplifier–a way to bring happiness skills to life when it matters most.

As we work through this chapter, remember that you already have the tools and the roadmap. Power-Ups are your next step—your way to create immediate meaningful momentum. Let's explore how you can use them to lead with intention and make happiness your most powerful leadership skill.

YOU MUST START WHERE YOU ARE.

Before using Power-Ups, it's essential to understand where you are right now in terms of energy and engagement. I always begin with a 24-point assessment rooted in the Eight Pillars of Happiness.

This assessment provides a powerful benchmark for understanding your strengths and growth areas, both personally and within your team. Are you thriving in Confidence but struggling with Gratitude? Are your team dynamics strong in Curiosity but lacking in Authenticity? By uncovering these patterns, you can effectively target the areas where Power-Ups will have the biggest impact.

What makes this assessment so effective is its foundation in The Eight Pillars themselves. It works seamlessly on an individual, team and organizational level because it gets to the heart of what drives energy, engagement and impact. When you measure against these metrics, you're not looking at surface-level symptoms—you're pinpointing what's working and what's not at the foundational level of happiness and human flourishing. And once you know that—once you can see your specific strengths and challenges—you can design solutions that meet them directly.

But it's important to note that this process isn't just about identifying gaps. It's also about celebrating your successes. Recognizing what you and your team are already doing well creates a dopamine boost—that's the brain's reward chemical—that energizes you to keep the momentum going. Progress motivates progress. And as you repeat the assessment over time, you'll see tangible improvements that reinforce your commitment to leading with happiness at the center.

So whether you're assessing yourself, your team or your entire organization, this tool gives you the clarity to take intentional, targeted action. Please remember that it's not about perfection. It's about progress—building on what's already strong and strategically addressing what needs attention. With this clarity, you will be able to design Power-Ups that amplify your energy, unlock new possibilities and keep you and your team moving forward.

Let me share an example of how one team used the assessment to identify their strengths and challenges, leading to meaningful Power-Ups that drove lasting impact.

USING DATA TO TARGET AND TRANSFORM A TEAM'S CHALLENGES.

When a global engineering firm reached out for help, their high-achieving employees were struggling. External stressors—international crises, a toxic election climate and uncertainty—had drained engagement and fractured communication. They wanted change but didn't know where to start.

That's what great leaders do—they ask for help. We began with an assessment, revealing strengths in Curiosity and Purpose, but struggles with Feeling, Authenticity and Compassion. Stress and uncertainty had eroded trust, leaving employees feeling unsupported.

Living It: Armed with this insight, we designed two Power-Up sessions focused on rebuilding trust, psychological safety and empathy. Through active listening, storytelling and group communication norms, the team practiced real-world strategies to strengthen connection.

Impact: The transformation was clear. Employees felt more connected, valued and better equipped to navigate challenges together. Their strengths in Purpose and Curiosity became even more powerful when combined with renewed trust and empathy—giving them sustainable tools for lasting change.

This is a powerful example of how Happy Leaders take intentional steps to strengthen their teams. By using data from the Eight Pillars and tailoring Power-Ups to meet specific challenges, Happy Leaders transform workplace dynamics and unlock new levels of success—even in the face of uncertainty.

SO WHAT EXACTLY ARE POWER-UPS?

Power-Ups are intentional action-oriented practices designed to help you recharge, refocus and realign your energy. They're simple, accessible and incredibly powerful, enabling you to respond to challenges, reset your mindset and amplify energy in real time.

Think of Power-Ups as the fuel that keeps you going. Just as athletes rely on hydration breaks or musicians take time to tune their instruments, Power-Ups are there to keep you sharp and aligned. These energy boosts radiate outward to impact every aspect of your life and leadership, helping you sustain positive engagement and drive meaningful outcomes.

What makes Power-Ups so versatile is their adaptability—they can be applied anywhere. At work, Power-Ups help Happy Leaders design cultures that energize rather than drain and cultivate environments where creativity and collaboration thrive. At home, they become rituals that ground you in self-care or reframe your perspective during challenging moments. And in relationships, Power-Ups are tools for rediscovering joy, strengthening connections and deepening empathy.

Happy Leaders use Power-Ups to supercharge positive energy and build the momentum they need to succeed. Whether you're brainstorming with your team, navigating a difficult conversation at home or simply taking a moment to reset your own energy, these practices create the space for you to show up as your best self.

Here's how it might look in action.

You notice a trend in your team—Thursday afternoons are always a slump. Productivity halts, the energy of the room nosedives and no one seems engaged with their work. You also know that there's a standing company-wide meeting on Thursday mornings, which could be contributing to this lull. As a Happy Leader, you recognize that an energy shift is needed for your team to show up at their best.

So you decide to implement a tailored Power-Up—a round-robin celebration where team members take turns rapid-firing gratitude for their colleagues. It takes just 10 minutes, but the impact is transformative. The shared appreciation and positive focus energize the team, resetting the tone for the rest of the day. Productivity picks up, collaboration becomes more fluid and the mood shifts from sluggish to motivated.

This is the power of Power-Ups—they're quick actions with outsized effects, helping you lead with intentionality and purpose.

THERE ARE THREE MAIN TYPES OF POWER-UPS.

To make Power-Ups practical, I organize them into three core categories. This approach helps you understand which area of your life as a Happy Leader needs an energy boost. By breaking them down into focused categories, it becomes easier to identify where to start, where to focus your attention and which Power-Ups will have the most impact.

Whether you're looking to supercharge your energy at home, enhance collaboration at work or strengthen relationships with others, this structure ensures that the Power-Ups are tailored to your specific needs. Each of these areas—Home, Work and Relationships—represents a key domain of a Happy Leader's life, where happiness and energy intersect, influencing how you engage.

◇ **Home**: Power-Ups that recharge your energy and help you align with purpose in your personal life.

◇ **Work**: Power-Ups that foster engagement, collaboration and creativity in professional settings.

◇ **Relationships:** Power-Ups that deepen connection and build trust with others.

These categories reflect the areas of life where happiness has the greatest impact. On average, people spend one-third of their lives—roughly 90,000 hours—at work. At the same time, the Harvard Study of Adult Development, one of the longest-running happiness studies in history, reveals that strong relationships are the single most consistent predictor of happiness and well-being[26]. In other words, the quality of our connections has a huge impact on how fulfilled we feel.

While these three areas may seem like separate domains, you've likely experienced how deeply interconnected they really are. What happens in one area of your life inevitably affects the others. When you feel drained at home, that energy comes with you to work, influencing your focus and interactions there. Similarly, a lack of meaningful connections can erode your sense of purpose, impacting both your personal and professional life.

So by organizing Power-Ups into these three categories, you're able to focus on what matters most in the areas where you spend the majority of your time. These practices can help boost energy in the moment and create an impact across all areas of your life. When you feel more grounded at home, you show up at work with greater clarity and confidence. When you foster meaningful relationships, you bring that sense of connection into every interaction, from leading your team to supporting your community.

Power-Ups aren't isolated actions. They are tools for building momentum in the spaces where life unfolds. By intentionally incorporating them at home, at work and in your relationships, you're designing an environment where happiness becomes a shared experience that inspires everyone to contribute at their best.

Before jumping into specific Power-Ups, let's take a moment to reflect on where you currently stand as a leader. This simplified assessment is designed to give you a snapshot of your energy and alignment with The Eight Pillars across the three key domains of your life: work, home and relationships.

Use it as a tool to pinpoint areas where you're thriving and identify opportunities for growth. This exercise is quick but powerful—an intentional pause to help you focus on where you can make the greatest impact.

THE HAPPY LEADER SELF-ASSESSMENT

For each pillar, rate yourself on a scale from 1 to 10 (1 = I'm not aligned at all; 10 = I'm fully aligned and thriving). Consider how you're showing up in each domain—at home, at work and in your relationships.

CONFIDENCE	
Home	How confident am I in navigating challenges and supporting growth in my personal life?
Work	How confident do I feel in my abilities to lead and make decisions at work?
Relationships	How confident am I in communicating and building trust with others?

AUTHENTICITY	
Home	Do my daily actions and decisions align with my values?
Work	How authentically do I show up at work, aligned with my values and true self?
Relationships	How authentically do I connect with others in my relationships?
PURPOSE	
Home	How purposeful do I feel in how I spend my time and energy outside of work?
Work	How clear and connected am I to the purpose of my work?
Relationships	How intentional am I in building meaningful connections with others?
COMPASSION	
Home	How compassionate am I toward myself?
Work	How often do I show empathy and support to my colleagues and team members?
Relationships	How well do I extend kindness and understanding to those around me?

GRATITUDE	
Home	How often do I reflect on and appreciate the good in my personal life?
Work	How often do I express appreciation and notice the positives at work?
Relationships	How consistently do I show gratitude to those I care about?
CURIOSITY	
Home:	How curious am I about learning and growing in my personal life?
Work	How open am I to exploring new ideas and perspectives at work?
Relationships	How often do I approach my relationships with curiosity and a desire to understand?
OPTIMISM	
Home	How hopeful am I about the future?
Work	How optimistic am I about achieving goals and overcoming challenges at work?
Relationships	How optimistic am I about the potential for growth and connection in my relationships?

FEELING	
Home	How in tune am I with my feelings and their impact on my personal life?
Work	How well do I acknowledge and manage my emotions in the workplace?
Relationships	How comfortable am I with expressing and understanding emotions in my relationships?

Pillar	Work (1-10)	Home (1-10)	Relationships (1-10)
Confidence			
Authenticity			
Purpose			
Compassion			
Gratitude			
Curiosity			
Optimism			
Feeling			

HAPPINESS HUDDLE ☺

Looking at your scores, what stands out? Which areas are your greatest strengths? Where do you see the most opportunity for growth or support?

As with all things happiness-related, Power-Ups are not about perfection. They're about progress. As a Happy Leader, your focus isn't on eliminating every obstacle or always being on. Instead, it's about having actionable tools to improve your situation, no matter where you're starting. This mindset turns challenges into opportunities for growth and builds the momentum needed to sustain your energy and impact.

Progress builds Confidence. Small wins—like taking a Gratitude pause during a busy day or practicing deep breathing before a tough conversation—reinforce positive behavior. Each success releases dopamine, that all-powerful motivator that keeps you moving forward. Dr. Teresa Amabile's progress principle emphasizes that even incremental progress fuels motivation and engagement[27]. When you focus on simple, intentional Power-Ups, you're building Confidence and energy while staying aligned with your bigger goals.

Progress aligns with Purpose. When Power-Ups resonate with your core values, they don't just feel good—they feel meaningful. Purpose gives direction to your actions, turning Power-Ups into energy boosts rather than just extra tasks on your to-do list.

Self-compassion sustains momentum. Not every Power-Up will work perfectly, and that's okay. Dr. Kristin Neff's research shows that self-compassion helps us navigate setbacks by reducing self-criticism and encouraging learning[28]. When a Power-Up doesn't go as planned, give yourself grace. Adjust, experiment and try again. This mindset keeps you energized and models resilience for your team.

Authenticity strengthens your approach. Power-Ups work best when they reflect who you are. If a Power-Up aligns with your strengths and values—like journaling for a reflective thinker or a quick brainstorm for a creative type—it's more likely to stick. By staying authentic, Power-Ups become a natural extension of your leadership style rather than feeling forced or performative.

THE BEAUTY OF POWER-UPS LIES IN THEIR SIMPLICITY.

A Gratitude pause during a hectic day can shift your perspective. A moment of deep breathing before a tough conversation can help you show up with clarity and calm. When repeated, these actions add up, becoming habits that seamlessly integrate into your culture and environment.

Power-Ups are most transformative when they're woven into the rhythms of daily life. Their effectiveness comes from building momentum. Simple, intentional actions compound over time to create lasting energy and impact. Embedding Power-Ups into processes and systems you already use ensures they become effortless, enhancing your home, work and relationships.

Momentum starts with manageable, bite-sized steps. Dr. BJ Fogg, author of *Tiny Habits,* emphasizes that starting with smaller, easy-to-implement actions increases the likelihood of long-term success[29]. Pairing a Power-Up with an existing habit—like practicing Gratitude during your morning coffee or taking three deep breaths before opening your email—helps it become an automatic part of your routine. This habit-stacking technique ensures consistency without adding overwhelm.

Consistency is key and habits are its foundation. James Clear, author of *Atomic Habits,* explains that habits form through repetition and are reinforced by visible rewards[30]. For Happy Leaders, the reward is the immediate energy boost a Power-Up provides. Tracking your progress—

through a journal, app or simple reflection—helps reinforce these habits by celebrating their positive impact.

Momentum grows with every win, no matter how small. When you complete a Power-Up, your brain releases dopamine—the chemical that reinforces positive behavior and motivates you to repeat it. Ending your day with an Optimism practice, for instance, doesn't just lift your mood—it strengthens your commitment to practicing Optimism regularly. Sharing these wins with your team amplifies the effect, fostering a culture of collective progress and positive energy.

To sustain momentum, regularly assess which Power-Ups resonate most and deliver the greatest impact. For leaders, this means getting feedback from your team. Ask how Power-Ups influence their engagement, morale or creativity. Understanding their experiences strengthens the practice and ensures Power-Ups stay relevant to ever-evolving needs.

What happens at home affects work, and what happens in relationships impacts it all. The energy of Power-Ups transcend time and space, offering tools to create alignment across all areas of life. Practicing active listening during family conversations will naturally extend into your professional interactions, deepening trust and connection with your team. Recognizing the interconnectedness amplifies the value of Power-Ups and motivates consistent use across contexts.

This interconnectedness highlights the versatility of Power-Ups, but even with their simplicity and flexibility, it's natural to encounter barriers when introducing something new. Some leaders worry they don't have the time to fit additional practices into already busy schedules. Others might assume that implementing these practices requires a significant financial investment.

Power-Ups aren't distractions or luxuries. They're investments in energy. And as we learned in Chapter 2, energy drives impact. So think of Power-Ups as targeted energy boosts that give you and your team the fuel needed for maximum impact. When you pause for self-compassion, host a wild brainstorming session or celebrate wins with your team, you're not taking time away from productivity—you're creating the conditions for more of it.

Consider that a simple five-minute Power-Up can help reset focus, increase engagement and even prevent burnout. Research from the American Psychological Association shows that simple well-being practices improve productivity and reduce stress[31]. And when implemented thoughtfully, Power-Ups don't just benefit you—they amplify energy across your team, unlocking higher levels of collaboration and creativity.

And like I've said, it's important to start where you are—right now, in this moment. Power-Ups aren't about overhauling your day—or your team—overnight. Choose one that feels manageable today and build from there. With every small step, you're making progress, and progress is what fuels meaningful change.

POWER-UPS CREATE MEASURABLE IMPACT FOR PEOPLE AND ORGANIZATIONS.

Power-Ups deliver real, tangible results. Personally, they help you boost energy, sharpen focus and stay engaged. On a bigger scale, they make an even greater difference. Research from Gallup consistently shows that when people feel good, they do good work—leading to higher productivity, less absenteeism and stronger retention[32]. Happier, healthier teams are more innovative, adaptable and motivated to deliver high-quality results[33]. And that's what we want, right? Happy people making big impacts.

Happy Leaders use Power-Ups to create environments where teams can flourish. They bridge the gap between well-being and performance, aligning energy with impact. When you track metrics like engagement, morale and retention, the results are undeniable. These aren't fluffy, feel-good practices—they're practical tools that drive real success, proving that happiness and high performance go hand in hand.

We've already covered that happiness isn't static–it's a process, influenced by your choices, your environment and your mindset. Power-Ups give you the tools to navigate that process with clarity and purpose. They help you respond to challenges, connect more deeply with others and build the energy you need to make an impact.

More importantly, Power-Ups help you lead with happiness. As a Happy Leader, your energy and actions set the tone for your entire team. When you use Power-Ups, you're creating more trust, collaboration and motivation. This is how happiness becomes a multiplier, spreading from you to your team and beyond.

In the next three chapters, we'll explore Power-Ups tailored to the three key domains of your life—Home, Work and Relationships. You'll learn how to recharge your energy at home, spark collaboration at work and strengthen the relationships that matter most. Each chapter is packed with practical, actionable ideas to help you start small, gain momentum and create meaningful change where you need it most.

Let's get to it.

#TLDR: KEY TAKEAWAYS

1. **Power-Ups are targeted energy boosts.** Simple, actionable practices designed to recharge, refocus and realign energy exactly where and when it's needed.

2. **Start where you are.** Power-Ups aren't about overhauling your life overnight—they're about meeting yourself where you are now. Begin with one simple, manageable action and build from there.

3. **Happiness is a multiplier.** Power-Ups expand energy outward, fostering more engagement and impact across all areas of life.

ACTION SHOT ☆

Take the Happy Leader Self-Assessment and identify one area—Work, Home or Relationships—where you want to focus your energy this week. Choose a Power-Up aligned with that area and give it a try.

HAPPINESS HUDDLE ☺

Reflect on The Eight Pillars. Which one feels most aligned with your current strengths? Where could a targeted Power-Up help you spark meaningful progress and momentum?

CHAPTER 5

The Happy Leader at Home

"Peace begins at home."

— Eleanor Roosevelt

Your home is more than a place. It's the foundation where every aspect of your leadership begins. The energy you cultivate at home—whether it's peace, respect, hope or joy—becomes the energy you carry with you into the world. Home Power-Ups are intentional energy boosts designed to help you align with what you need most, when you need it.

These practices can relieve stress, promote mindfulness and strengthen your ability to lead with happiness and intention. A supportive home environment nurtures your physical and emotional well-being, creating a springboard for greater productivity, creativity and fulfillment. Research shows that such environments foster emotional balance, reduce stress and boost focus and decision-making[34].

By designing your home life to reflect the energy and values you want more of, you're creating a happier space for yourself and setting the tone for how you engage with your work, relationships and goals. And it all begins where it matters most—at home.

You can use Home Power-Ups to bring clarity and momentum into your life. Instead of rushing through the motions, choose a Power-Up that helps you pause and recharge, realigning yourself with Purpose. Intentional actions like practicing Gratitude, showing Compassion or carving out space for reflection ground you and sustain your energy for what matters most.

Rooted in evidence-based strategies, Home Power-Ups strengthen your capacity to lead with the positive energy needed to fuel engagement and impact. They aren't one-size-fits-all—they should be tailored to your unique needs, preferences and lifestyle. So whether you're creating a peaceful morning routine, prioritizing physical health or infusing joy into your day, Power-Ups allow you to focus on what feels most impactful to you.

When your Power-Ups align with your core values they become natural and sustainable habits rather than one-off actions. These targeted energy boosts elevate your well-being and energize how you show up in every other area of life.

In this chapter, we'll explore five categories of Home Power-Ups— Mindset, Health, Growth, Environment and Joy. Each category offers practical and impactful examples, along with strategies to help you design your own Power-Ups that align with your values and goals.

Home Power-Ups empower Happy Leaders to:

- Reduce stress while cultivating emotional balance

- Boost physical energy and vitality for greater resilience

- Strengthen personal growth and inspire meaningful development

- Create a supportive home environment that nurtures well-being

- Cultivate joyful moments and connections with loved ones

By integrating science-backed Power-Ups into your home life, you're build-ing a foundation of energy and impact that supports everything you do.

THE TIMING OF YOUR POWER-UPS IS JUST AS IMPORTANT AS THE POWER-UPS THEMSELVES.

By intentionally choosing when to use them, Power-Ups help you shift your energy, regain focus and ground yourself exactly when you need it most. Understanding the best timing for your needs ensures these practices create maximum impact in your home life.

Morning Power-Ups set the tone for the day. Mornings are a fresh start, offering an opportunity to begin with intention and clarity. A well-placed Power-Up in the morning prepares your mind and body for the day ahead, helping you feel centered and ready to tackle your priorities.

Midday Power-Ups provide a reset when energy dips. As the day progresses, stress and fatigue can build, and productivity often wanes. A midday Power-Up helps you pause, recharge and approach the rest of your day with renewed focus and energy.

Evening Power-Ups create space to unwind and reflect. The end of the day is a natural transition from activity to rest. Intentional evening Power-Ups help you release stress and cultivate calm, setting you up for restorative sleep.

Anytime Power-Ups are your on-the-go tools for real-time energy shifts. Life is unpredictable and moments of overwhelm or distraction can happen unexpectedly. Anytime Power-Ups offer quick, adaptable ways to ground yourself and reset energy wherever you are.

Aligning Power-Ups with key moments in your day creates a natural flow that supports your energy. Research underscores the benefits of timing practices to fit your body's natural rhythms. For example, practicing mindfulness in the morning can enhance focus and reduce stress hormones like cortisol, while physical movement in the afternoon helps restore alertness and boost mood.

The key is to experiment with timing to discover what works best for you. A morning Power-Up might help you feel grounded and proactive, while an evening ritual could be your favorite way to create peace after a busy day. With intentional timing, Power-Ups become an integral part of your routine.

HOME POWER-UPS ARE ALL ABOUT CREATING ENERGY AT HOME.

Home Power-Ups are designed to elevate your energy in ways that resonate with your unique needs and values. Let's explore the five categories of Home Power-Ups—Mindset, Health, Growth, Environment and Joy. For each, you'll discover specific Power-Ups tailored to help you enhance energy, reduce stress and intentionally align with your values and goals. These Power-Ups are designed to be simple, effective and easy to integrate into your daily routines.

Let's get started.

MINDSET POWER-UPS

Happy Leaders know that a clear, focused mind is essential for sustaining energy and creating meaningful impact. Why does this matter? A cluttered, stressed mind drains energy, making it harder to navigate challenges and connect effectively with others.

Mindset Power-Ups help you redirect your mental energy toward what truly matters. By creating space to respond intentionally rather than reacting impulsively, you lay the groundwork for meaningful contributions. According to the Energy-Impact Model, positive energy starts with a focused mindset—helping you tackle challenges, strengthen connections and build momentum in your home and beyond.

USE MINDSET POWER-UPS WHEN:

- You're feeling stuck or overwhelmed

- You need a confidence or motivation boost

- Life throws you a curveball and you need to reset

- You want to approach your day with more positivity and intention

Now, let's dive into some Mindset Power-Ups designed to help you cultivate energy, clarity and intention!

MINDSET POWER-UPS
Set the Vibe: Pick one word to guide your day (ex. "bold" or "calm").   **Happiness Pillars:** *Optimism, Purpose*
Plot Twist: Rewrite setbacks as plot twists that make your story epic.   **Happiness Pillars:** *Curiosity, Confidence*
Boost Mode: Say *I've got this*! every time doubt creeps in.   **Happiness Pillars:** *Confidence, Optimism*
Emotion Radar: Hit pause, name what you're feeling and own it.   **Happiness Pillars:** *Feeling, Authenticity, Compassion*

MINDSET POWER-UPS
Gratitude Snapshots: Write three things you're thankful for like captions on Instagram.   **Happiness Pillars:** *Gratitude, Optimism*
Future Flash: Close your eyes and picture yourself nailing that big goal.   **Happiness Pillars:** *Optimism, Purpose*
Win Tracker: Celebrate tiny victories with a fist pump or a happy dance.   **Happiness Pillars:** *Confidence, Gratitude*
Fail Forward: Treat every "oops" as a new badge in your life skills collection.   **Happiness Pillars:** *Curiosity, Confidence, Authenticity*
Find Your Fire: Ask yourself, *What's my why?* before diving into your to-dos.   **Happiness Pillars:** *Purpose, Authenticity*
Pep Talk: Give yourself a quick mirror high-five or a fist bump and say, *Let's do this!*   **Happiness Pillars:** *Compassion, Confidence, Feeling*

Now that your mind is clear and focused, it's time to turn your attention to your body. Just like a strong mindset fuels energy and impact, a healthy body ensures you have the stamina and resilience to show up as your best self.

Health Power-Ups are powerful actions that boost your physical energy and well-being, setting the foundation for peak performance in every area of life.

HEALTH POWER-UPS

Happy Leaders understand that physical energy is the fuel for resilience and clarity. Health Power-Ups prioritize your physical well-being, helping you feel strong, energized and ready to take on life's challenges.

Why is this so important? Your physical health directly impacts your energy levels, focus and mood. When your body feels drained, it's harder to show up fully in your personal life or leadership roles. Health Power-Ups help you create sustainable energy that aligns with the Energy-Impact Model, giving you the capacity to lead with purpose and positivity. By integrating them into your daily routine, you're not just taking care of your body—you're enhancing your ability to connect, grow and make a meaningful impact.

The benefits are supported by science—regular movement boosts endorphins, reduces stress and enhances cognitive function, while mindful eating promotes both physical and emotional well-being. Prioritizing sleep, hydration and nutrition is linked to improved decision-making and emotional regulation, allowing you to approach your day with clarity and balance.

USE HEALTH POWER-UPS WHEN:

- You're feeling low on energy or motivation

- Stress or tension is taking a toll on your body

- You want to strengthen the connection between your physical and emotional well-being

- You're ready to make small changes for long-term vitality

Let's dive into some Health Power-Ups designed to help you recharge and refocus your energy for maximum impact.

HEALTH POWER-UPS

Hydration Hero: Start your day with a full glass of water to wake up your body and mind.

Happiness Pillars: *Feeling, Purpose*

Move to Energize: Do 10 minutes of movement—stretch, dance or walk around the block.

Happiness Pillars: *Optimism, Confidence*

Snack Smart: Swap one processed snack for a whole food.

Happiness Pillars: *Gratitude, Purpose*

Power Down: Go phone-free before bed to improve sleep quality.

Happiness Pillars: *Authenticity, Feeling*

Deep Breather: Take five deep belly breaths to reset your energy during stressful moments.

Happiness Pillars: *Compassion, Confidence*

Sunshine Boost: Spend 10 minutes outside to soak up natural light and recharge.

Happiness Pillars: *Optimism, Gratitude*

Mindful Munching: Eat one meal slowly, savoring every bite

Happiness Pillars: *Feeling, Curiosity*

Stretch It Out: Take a two-minute stretch break to release tension and improve circulation.

Happiness Pillars: *Confidence, Purpose*

HEALTH POWER-UPS
Sleep Ritual: Create a calming bedtime routine with a book, tea or relaxing music. **Happiness Pillars:** *Feeling, Compassion, Gratitude*
Energy Check: Pause to ask yourself, *What does my body need right now?* and act on it. **Happiness Pillars:** *Authenticity, Curiosity, Feeling*

With your body recharged and energized, it's time to focus on your personal and professional growth. Just as physical energy fuels resilience, intentional growth fuels innovation, confidence and a sense of purpose.

Growth Power-Ups are designed to help you stretch your mind, expand your horizons and tap into your full potential. By integrating these into your daily life, you'll cultivate the skills and mindset needed to continuously evolve and thrive.

GROWTH POWER-UPS

Happy Leaders know that growth is essential for long-term fulfillment and impact. Growth Power-Ups encourage self-improvement, spark curiosity and help you build the mental and emotional skills you need for maximum impact.

Growth is about expanding your perspective, deepening your self-awareness and aligning your actions with your values. These Power-Ups connect directly to the Energy-Impact Model by fostering emotional energy and intellectual clarity, which amplify your ability to make a meaningful difference.

USE THESE WHEN:

- You want to spark new ideas and creativity
- You're seeking clarity about your next steps
- You feel ready to step outside your comfort zone
- You want to build resilience and self-confidence

Let's look at some Growth Power-Ups designed to help you fuel personal development and inspire new perspectives.

GROWTH POWER-UPS

Daily Discovery: Spend 15 minutes learning something new—read, listen or watch.

Happiness Pillars: *Curiosity, Confidence*

Dream Mapping: Write down one big dream and list three small steps to start.

Happiness Pillars: *Purpose, Optimism*

Reflect & Reset: Journal about a recent challenge and what you learned from it.

Happiness Pillars: *Authenticity, Curiosity*

Feedback Focus: Ask someone you trust for one piece of constructive feedback.

Happiness Pillars: *Confidence, Compassion*

Skill Sharpening: Dedicate time to improve a skill you've always wanted to master.

Happiness Pillars: *Curiosity, Purpose*

GROWTH POWER-UPS

Perspective Shift: Read or watch something from a viewpoint different from your own.
Happiness Pillars: *Curiosity, Feeling*

Goal Reboot: Revisit one of your goals and adjust it to better align with your values.
Happiness Pillars: *Purpose, Authenticity*

Progress Party: List three ways you've grown in the past year.
Happiness Pillars: *Gratitude, Confidence*

Connection Boost: Reach out to someone who inspires you and start a conversation.
Happiness Pillars: *Compassion, Curiosity, Confidence*

Playtime: Take 10 minutes to play—build, doodle or make up a silly game.
Happiness Pillars: *Optimism, Curiosity, Feeling*

As you nurture personal growth and expand your mindset, it's important to consider the space around you. Your environment plays a crucial role in supporting your energy, focus and overall well-being.

Environment Power-Ups are designed to help you create spaces that inspire, energize and align with your goals. By making intentional changes to your surroundings, you can set the stage for creativity and positive energy in every aspect of your life.

ENVIRONMENT POWER-UPS

Happy Leaders know that the spaces around them profoundly influence their mindset, energy and ability to focus. Every element—color, design, patterns, textures, greenery and sunlight—plays a role in shaping your energy, whether you're consciously aware of it or not.

Environment Power-Ups transform your home into a supportive, energizing space where you can recharge and reenergize. By aligning your surroundings with your values and goals, you create an environment that nurtures clarity, calm and creativity—enhancing your ability to lead effectively.

Why is this important? Because the spaces we inhabit either fuel or drain our energy. Chaotic or cluttered environments increase stress and hinder focus, while intentional, organized spaces promote emotional balance, creativity and productivity. Your home can become an energy sanctuary—a space that fuels exactly what you need to feel inspired and empowered.

USE THESE WHEN:

- You feel overstimulated or distracted

- Your environment doesn't match your energy or goals

- You need a fresh perspective to spark creativity

- You're ready to create a space that recharges and inspires you

Here are some Environment Power-Ups designed to help optimize your spaces and elevate your energy.

ENVIRONMENT POWER-UPS

Declutter Blitz: Pick one area (like your desk or kitchen counter) and clear it completely.

Happiness Pillars: *Gratitude, Confidence*

Color Boost: Add pops of energizing colors (yellow, anyone?) to your workspace or living area.

Happiness Pillars: *Optimism, Curiosity*

Plant Power: Bring nature indoors with a new plant—or give your current greenery some TLC.

Happiness Pillars: *Feeling, Gratitude, Compassion*

Sunlight Reset: Spend time in your sunniest room or open the blinds to let natural light in.

Happiness Pillars: *Optimism, Gratitude*

Texture Therapy: Incorporate soft textures like blankets or rugs to create a cozy, calming vibe.

Happiness Pillars: *Feeling, Compassion*

Visual Alignment: Rearrange one area to reflect your current goals or values.

Happiness Pillars: *Authenticity, Purpose*

Sensory Shift: Add a scent you love—candles or fresh flowers—for an instant mood boost.

Happiness Pillars: *Feeling, Optimism*

Soundtrack Shift: Play music that matches the mood you want— calm, focused or joyful.

Happiness Pillars: *Curiosity, Optimism*

ENVIRONMENT POWER-UPS

Clear Your Path: Keep walkways and frequently used spaces clutter-free for ease and flow.

Happiness Pillars: *Confidence, Purpose*

Nature-Inspired: Add natural materials like wood, stone or woven textures to ground your space.

Happiness Pillars: *Gratitude, Feeling*

With your environment optimized to fuel clarity and calm, it's time to focus on what truly lights you up. Joy Power-Ups remind us that happiness isn't just a result of success—it's a driving force behind it.

JOY POWER-UPS

Happy Leaders understand joy as a vital source of energy. Joy Power-Ups are playful and inject fun and positivity into your life. They remind you not to take things too seriously and provide a powerful reset when stress or routine starts to weigh you down.

Joy is a catalyst for effective leadership. Engaging in joyful activities reduces stress, strengthens relationships and boosts creative thinking.

USE THESE WHEN:

- Stress feels overwhelming, and you need a quick mood lift

- Your daily routine starts to feel too heavy or monotonous

- You want to strengthen connections and create meaningful moments with loved ones

- You're ready to embrace more playfulness and positivity in your life

Joy Power-Ups infuse life with positivity, enhancing your energy and uplifting everyone around you.

JOY POWER-UPS

Dance Party: Put on your favorite song and dance like no one's watching.
Happiness Pillars: *Optimism, Feeling*

Laugh Track: Watch a funny video or share a joke with someone you love.
Happiness Pillars: *Feeling, Compassion*

Forced Fun: Spend 10 minutes doing something playful—draw, sing or build with Legos!
Happiness Pillars: *Curiosity, Optimism*

Surprise and Delight: Do something unexpected for someone else, like leaving a kind note.
Happiness Pillars: *Gratitude, Compassion*

Memory Lane: Look through old photos that make you smile.
Happiness Pillars: *Gratitude, Feeling*

Joy Jar: Write down one joyful moment from your day and add it to a jar for future smiles.
Happiness Pillars: *Gratitude, Optimism*

JOY POWER-UPS

Restful Recess: Take a walk outside and find something beautiful to admire.

Happiness Pillars: *Curiosity, Feeling*

Mirror High-Five: Give yourself a high-five in the mirror and celebrate a small win.

Happiness Pillars: *Gratitude, Confidence*

Movie Night Magic: Watch an old favorite or a feel-good film with family or friends.

Happiness Pillars: *Feeling, Compassion*

Creativity Corner: Try something creative just for fun—and without worrying about the outcome.

Happiness Pillars: *Curiosity, Optimism, Authenticity*

Now that you've explored ways to spark joy and infuse positivity into your life, it's time to take the next step and design your own Power-Ups. Customizing Power-Ups allows you to align them even more closely with your unique needs, goals and values.

TAKE CONTROL OF YOUR HOME WITH DIY (DESIGN IT YOURSELF) POWER-UPS.

Creating your own Power-Ups is even more empowering. This framework will help you address your unique needs and align with what truly matters to you, making you the architect of your own happiness. As a Happy Leader, you already have all the tools—you just need to use them intentionally in ways that resonate most with you.

Start by asking yourself—*How might I use this moment or space to create more positive energy for myself?* With this simple question, you can design Power-Ups that seamlessly fit your life, enhancing your day and impacting everyone around you.

Identify the pillars most that align with your current needs. What do you need most right now? Reflect on the Eight Pillars of Happiness and consider which ones align with your current situation. Maybe Gratitude could help you focus on the good amidst challenges or Confidence could help you tackle a daunting project. Often, combining pillars—like Curiosity with Compassion—can inspire creative solutions that fuel the energy you need.

Focus on the impact you want to create. Be specific about the outcome you're aiming for. Are you looking to lower stress or boost your energy for the day ahead? When you're clear about the impact you want, you can design a Power-Up that directly supports it, making it easier to integrate and sustain.

Keep it simple to make it sustainable. The beauty of Power-Ups lies in their simplicity. They're not about adding more to your plate—they're about enhancing what you're already doing. When your Power-Up is manageable and fits naturally into your already busy day, it becomes a small but powerful tool to fuel your energy and amplify your impact.

LET'S BRING THIS TO LIFE.

Let's say that evenings often feel like a chaotic sprint from dinner to bedtime, leaving you drained and unprepared for the next day. To shift the energy, you could design a Power-Up to bring calm, focus and gratefulness into your nightly routine, aligning with the pillars of Gratitude, Purpose and Feeling.

Your new reflection ritual begins after you've tidied up for the day. You take ten quiet minutes in your favorite chair with a notebook. You start by jotting down three wins from your day—small victories like handling a tough conversation or carving out time for self-care. Next, you list one thing you're grateful for and why it matters. You end with a simple intention for tomorrow—*I will make space for creativity.*

This DIY Power-Up creates a sense of closure for your day, allowing you to process emotions and set the stage for purposeful action tomorrow. Over time, it becomes an anchor, helping you transition from the hustle of the day into restful sleep while energizing you for what lies ahead.

TAKE CHARGE OF YOUR HAPPINESS.

This Design it Yourself framework gives Happy Leaders like you the power to transform everyday moments into meaningful ones. By aligning your Power-Ups with the Eight Pillars and creating more positive energy, you're designing a life where happiness helps fuel everything you do.

The best part? Every Power-Up you create is uniquely yours, tailored to fit your values, goals and needs. As a Happy Leader, this is your superpower—turning intentional actions into tools that amplify your energy, deepen your connections and inspire those around you to flourish.

YOUR HOME SHOULD BE A SANCTUARY.

It should be a place where energy is restored, creativity is sparked and happiness grows. By intentionally using Power-Ups, you can make it the energy-giving space you need for living the life you love.

As you master creating energy in your home, imagine carrying this same intentionality into your work. In the next chapter, we'll head into the workplace, where your energy drives innovation, collaboration and meaningful impact. You'll learn how to use Power-Ups to supercharge your team's engagement and productivity, ensuring that happiness becomes a strategic advantage. Imagine transforming meetings, projects and collaborations—leading with the positive energy that inspires your team and elevates your impact.

#TLDR: KEY TAKEAWAYS

1. **Your home is your energy sanctuary.** Intentionally designed spaces and routines reduce stress, boost focus and nurture your physical and emotional well-being.

2. **Power-Ups transform ordinary moments.** By aligning intentional actions with the Eight Pillars of Happiness, Power-Ups help build sustainable habits that amplify your impact at home and beyond.

3. **Timing is everything.** Morning, Midday, Evening and Anytime Power-Ups allow you to align your energy with your needs, exactly when you need it most.

ACTION SHOT ☆

Take the DIY Power-Up framework for a spin. Identify two Pillars that resonate with your current needs this week at home and design a simple Power-Up to address them.

HAPPINESS HUDDLE ☺

What is one small change—either in your routines or your space—that could immediately enhance your energy and well-being at home?

CHAPTER 6

The Happy Leader at Work

"Leadership is not about being in charge.
It is about taking care of those in your charge."

— Indra Nooyi

Work is where we bring our energy, ideas and efforts to life. For Happy Leaders, the workplace is a space to inspire, connect and drive meaningful impact. Work Power-Ups are tools to help you cultivate the energy everyone needs to flourish in this space.

Your energy is your leadership currency and the way you manage it has a profound effect on your team's success. Whether you lead a remote team, manage cross-functional groups or work within a hybrid structure, Power-Ups are adaptable to your unique circumstances. Research underscores that leaders who prioritize happiness and meaning not only perform better themselves but also positively impact their teams—exactly what leadership needs today.

This chapter is all about using the science to enhance team dynamics, spark creativity and align with organizational goals. When you integrate Power-Ups at work, you're creating a culture where everyone can contribute at their best.

As we covered in depth in Chapter 2, happiness creates success and drives meaningful results. And as you remember from our Energy-Impact Model, positive energy at the personal level affects impact at the organizational level. So when you bring positive energy to your work, it boosts productivity, collaboration and innovation across the board. Let's quickly re-ground ourselves in the research that backs the impact this has in the workplace.

Happiness boosts productivity. A happy brain gets more done. Research by Shawn Achor, author of *The Happiness Advantage*, found that positive emotions increase productivity by 31%, improve accuracy by 19% and enhance creativity threefold[35]. When your team feels supported and valued, they perform at their best, delivering stronger results for the organization.

Happiness increases engagement. Engaged employees are enthusiastic and connected to their work, and that energy drives success. Gallup research shows that highly engaged employees are 21% more productive and 17% more profitable[36]. Engagement grows in a culture that prioritizes recognition, purpose and trust—key components of workplace happiness.

Happiness builds resilience and lowers burnout. Resilience is a must in today's fast-paced work environments. Positive emotions help you bounce back from challenges and think more clearly in tough situations. As you may recall from Chapter 2, Dr. Barbara Fredrickson's work shows that positive emotions broaden your perspective, improve problem-solving and help you recover from stress faster[37]. Without these benefits, burnout, absenteeism and turnover can skyrocket.

Happiness sparks creativity and innovation. Positive work environments lead to better ideas. Dr. Amy Edmondson's research on psychological safety shows that people are more willing to share creative solutions when they feel safe and supported[38]. Studies published in *Psychological Science* confirm that positive emotions enhance cognitive flexibility, helping you and your team think in fresh and innovative ways[39].

Happiness strengthens trust and collaboration. Happiness is the foundation for strong, effective teams. Studies in the *Journal of Organizational Behavior* show that happiness improves relationships and creates a sense of camaraderie[40]. When you model positivity and empathy, you build trust and foster an environment where collaboration thrives.

When you intentionally design for happiness at work, you're creating a workplace where people flourish. That means better results for you, your team and your organization. Let's explore how Happy Leaders use Power-Ups to make that happen.

USE POWER-UPS AT THE RIGHT TIME TO MAXIMIZE THEIR IMPACT.

Every workday has its rhythm—natural ebbs and flows of energy, focus and connection. As a Happy Leader, understanding these rhythms gives you an edge. By aligning Power-Ups with key moments, you can create the energy, focus and engagement needed for everyone on your team.

Arrival Power-Ups help set the tone for the day. The beginning of the workday is a powerful moment to set the tone for everyone. Whether you're stepping into the office, logging in remotely or starting a team meeting, this is your opportunity to create clarity and focus. A well-timed Power-Up can foster a positive and intentional atmosphere, setting the stage for a productive, focused day.

Midday Power-Ups help recharge and stay focused. As the day progresses, natural energy dips and mounting responsibilities can make it harder for everyone to sustain focus. Midday Power-Ups provide the reset you and your team need to regain momentum. Taking intentional action to recharge at this time can help the entire group approach the afternoon with renewed energy and effectiveness.

Meeting Power-Ups encourage collaboration and engagement. Meetings are pivotal moments in any workday, offering opportunities for alignment and connection. But without intention, they can easily become an energy drain. Incorporating Power-Ups during meetings can help keep everyone energized and engaged.

End-of-day Power-Ups create closure and prepare people for what's next. The close of the workday is an opportunity to reflect and celebrate. This is the moment to acknowledge progress, share wins and ensure everyone feels a sense of accomplishment. Using Power-Ups at this time can help your team leave work with clarity and pride, setting the stage for a strong start tomorrow.

By timing Power-Ups to the workday's flow, you amplify team energy. This strengthens their ability to stay engaged and productive. Whether it's setting the tone in the morning, resetting after lunch or reflecting at the end of the day, the right Power-Up at the right time makes a big impact on collective success.

WORK POWER-UPS CREATE MORE ENERGY, ENGAGEMENT AND IMPACT.

They are intentionally designed to elevate your team's energy and drive meaningful results. In this section, we'll explore five categories of Work Power-Ups—Productivity, Engagement, Innovation, Performance and Resilience. Each category addresses specific needs in the workplace, from sharpening focus and building collaboration to sparking creativity and strengthening adaptability.

But before we jump in, let's meet Susan.

HOW POWER-UPS SUPERCHARGED SUSAN'S PERFORMANCE.

My client Susan* works for a company that understands the power of designing for happiness at work. Her role in customer service is critical to the company's success and she approaches it with patience and grace. Susan's ability to connect with customers sets her apart, earning her repeat requests and glowing feedback.

Her manager knows what a valuable asset Susan is to the team—when she's able to show up at her best. Outside of work, Susan faces unique challenges. Her mobility is limited due to physical health challenges, requiring her to carefully manage her energy and routines to stay at her peak. She knows her most productive hours, understands when she needs rest and recognizes what she needs to show up at her best.

Living It: Susan's leaders use targeted Power-Ups to align her work environment with her needs. They adjusted her schedule to match her most productive hours, introduced accommodations to reduce physical strain and created space for open communication. These actions empower Susan to bring her best self to work consistently, allowing her to focus her energy on delivering exceptional customer experiences with compassion.

Impact: The impact of these adjustments is undeniable. Susan feels supported and valued, which allows her to show up fully for her customers. Her compassion fosters trust, driving customer loyalty and repeat business. Her manager has seen firsthand how creating the right conditions for Susan's success translates into exceptional team performance.

*Name changed for client privacy.

Susan's story highlights how Work Power-Ups can create a significant business advantage. When leaders use intentional actions to listen, accommodate and align with their team's needs, they unlock higher engagement, stronger loyalty and better results at every level.

PRODUCTIVITY POWER-UPS

Happy Leaders know that team productivity isn't just about individual contributions—it's about creating the conditions for collaboration and focus. Team Productivity Power-Ups help your team align on priorities, eliminate bottlenecks and sustain momentum.

Why is this so important? Disconnected efforts, unclear priorities and a lack of structure can leave teams feeling overwhelmed and unproductive. Productivity Power-Ups help your team stay focused on shared goals, streamline workflows and build the trust and clarity needed to succeed. When your team's efforts are aligned, everyone can contribute their best, ensuring that productivity translates into meaningful progress.

Clear communication and goal-setting enhance team performance, while structured collaboration improves decision-making and reduces inefficiencies. Productivity Power-Ups create a culture of accountability and focus, driving results while fostering team cohesion.

USE PRODUCTIVITY POWER-UPS WHEN:

- Your team feels scattered or unfocused

- Priorities are unclear, and momentum is stalling

- Bottlenecks or inefficiencies are slowing progress

- There's a big project and the team needs to deliver on time

- Looming deadlines require focused effort

Now let's explore some Productivity Power-Ups designed to help your team work smarter and achieve more together.

PRODUCTIVITY POWER-UPS
Mission Control: Huddle to align on the team's top three priorities and tackle any blockers. **Happiness Pillars:** *Confidence, Purpose*
Focus Fortress: Block out shared deep work hours for the entire team to tackle their most important tasks without interruptions. **Happiness Pillars:** *Authenticity, Confidence*
Role Roulette: Swap roles for an hour to approach tasks with fresh eyes and gain new perspectives. **Happiness Pillars:** *Curiosity, Gratitude*
Win Streak: Dedicate five minutes in meetings to share team wins—big or small—and build momentum for the next milestone. **Happiness Pillars:** *Gratitude, Optimism*
Feedback Flow: Host a quick chat where team members share constructive feedback to strengthen collaboration and performance. **Happiness Pillars:** *Compassion, Confidence*
Compass Check: Organize a weekly team sync to revisit shared objectives and ensure everyone's rowing in the same direction. **Happiness Pillars:** *Purpose, Curiosity*
Energy Sync: Map out each member's peak energy times and plan critical tasks or discussions around collective strengths. **Happiness Pillars:** *Authenticity, Feeling*

PRODUCTIVITY POWER-UPS
Checkpoint Challenge: Break big projects into smaller milestones and use creative team check-ins to celebrate progress. **Happiness Pillars:** *Confidence, Gratitude*
Agenda Accelerator: Transform meetings by crowdsourcing agendas and assigning clear outcomes before they begin. **Happiness Pillars:** *Purpose, Confidence*
Collective Recharge: Take short, collective breaks (think 10-minute walks or team-led stretch sessions) to recharge and re-center together. **Happiness Pillars:** *Feeling, Optimism*

With productivity optimized, it's time to deepen team connections and boost alignment. Next we'll explore Engagement Power-Ups to ensure your team stays motivated, connected and energized for the road ahead.

ENGAGEMENT POWER-UPS

Happy Leaders know that engagement is the fuel that powers team success. When team members feel connected, motivated and aligned with their purpose, their energy transforms into meaningful impact. Engagement Power-Ups are designed to foster a sense of belonging, increase motivation and deepen commitment within your team.

Because research shows exactly that—engaged employees are more productive, resilient and innovative. They're fully invested in the mission and in each other. As we saw earlier with the Energy-Impact Model, engagement creates a flow of energy that amplifies collaboration and drives results.

By integrating these Power-Ups into your leadership practices you'll cultivate an environment where your team collaborates and finds fulfillment in their work.

USE ENGAGEMENT POWER-UPS WHEN:

- Team morale feels low, and motivation is lacking

- Members feel disconnected or out of sync with one another

- You want to strengthen trust and alignment around shared goals

- Your team needs a boost in collaboration to tackle new challenges

Now let's dive into some specific Engagement Power-Ups designed to supercharge your team's connection and commitment.

ENGAGEMENT POWER-UPS
Story Swap: Pair team members to share short stories about something that made them proud. **Happiness Pillars:** *Confidence, Gratitude*
Emoji Check-In: To kickoff meetings, have everyone share an emoji that reflects their mood. **Happiness Pillars:** *Authenticity, Curiosity*
Shout-Out Spotlight: Dedicate a moment during team meetings to highlight someone's recent contributions. **Happiness Pillars:** *Gratitude, Confidence*
Purpose Post-It: Everyone writes one way their work connects to the bigger mission and sticks it on a shared wall or virtual board. **Happiness Pillars:** *Purpose, Gratitude*

ENGAGEMENT POWER-UPS

Random Acts of Fun: Surprise your team with something unexpected—like trivia questions, a meme of the week or a silly prize for no reason at all.

Happiness Pillars: *Optimism, Curiosity*

Collab Challenge: Assign two team members a mini-project to complete together in 15 minutes.

Happiness Pillars: *Confidence, Compassion*

Kudos Chain: One team member shares gratitude, passing it on until everyone is recognized.

Happiness Pillars: *Gratitude, Compassion*

Idea Blitz: Set a 10-minute timer and brainstorm solutions to a challenge together, encouraging bold and creative suggestions.

Happiness Pillars: *Curiosity, Confidence*

Mission Mini-Break: Pause mid-project to discuss how the current work aligns with the team's values or mission.

Happiness Pillars: *Purpose, Authenticity*

Energy Snapshot: During long meetings, take a 2-minute break for everyone to rate their energy on a scale of 1–10 and suggest quick ways to recharge if needed.

Happiness Pillars: *Feeling, Compassion*

With your team engaged and aligned, it's time to channel that energy into creativity and fresh ideas. In the next section, we'll explore Innovation Power-Ups—practices that spark curiosity, encourage bold thinking and unleash your team's full potential to solve complex challenges and drive meaningful progress.

INNOVATION POWER-UPS

Innovation fuels both growth and adaptability. It's about solving problems, improving processes and staying ahead in a competitive marketplace. Happy Leaders know that fostering innovation requires consistently creating the conditions for creativity and experimentation to thrive.

Research shows that companies prioritizing innovation are more likely to outperform their peers in revenue growth and market share. Innovation energizes teams, drives progress and aligns purpose with impact. It's not just about generating ideas—it's about turning those ideas into actionable solutions that move the needle.

USE INNOVATION POWER-UPS WHEN:

- Your team is stuck in old ways of thinking and needs a fresh perspective

- A complex challenge requires out-of-the-box solutions

- You want to encourage risk-taking and bold experimentation

- Team energy is low and you want to spark creativity and collaboration

Let's look at some Power-Ups that supercharge creativity and innovation.

INNOVATION POWER-UPS

Wild Brainstorms: Dedicate time for blue-sky thinking where no idea is too out there. The wilder, the better!

Happiness Pillars: *Curiosity, Optimism*

Prototype Party: Build quick, scrappy prototypes or mockups to bring ideas to life and test them in real time.

Happiness Pillars: *Confidence, Purpose*

INNOVATION POWER-UPS

Walking Think Tanks: Take team brainstorms on the move—walk around the office or outdoors to encourage fresh ideas.

Happiness Pillars: *Curiosity, Feeling*

Idea Roulette: Team members combine random concepts or problems to spark creative solutions.

Happiness Pillars: *Curiosity, Authenticity*

Prototype Postmortem: Analyze failed ideas with curiosity to identify what worked and what can inspire future success.

Happiness Pillars: *Curiosity, Confidence*

Curiosity Catalyst: Invite a guest speaker from outside your industry to inspire new perspectives and approaches.

Happiness Pillars: *Curiosity, Gratitude*

30-Minute Blitz: Set a timer and work collaboratively to generate as many ideas as possible for a specific problem.

Happiness Pillars: *Confidence, Curiosity*

Rapid Refinement: Take one bold idea and spend a set time refining it into a viable solution.

Happiness Pillars: *Purpose, Confidence*

Reverse Brainstorming: Ask, *What would make this problem worse?* and then brainstorm solutions to prevent those scenarios.

Happiness Pillars: *Curiosity, Authenticity*

Idea Wall: Create a physical or digital space where team members can post ideas, feedback or inspirations at any time.

Happiness Pillars: *Curiosity, Purpose*

With fresh ideas flowing and bold solutions taking shape, it's time to shift gears toward execution. Next we'll look at Performance Power-Ups—strategies to turn innovative thinking into impactful results while maximizing efficiency and effectiveness.

PERFORMANCE POWER-UPS

Happy Leaders know that exceptional performance isn't about constant hustle—it's about aligning energy, focus and resources for maximum impact. Performance Power-Ups are intentional practices that optimize productivity, enhance focus and create a rhythm of success that is both sustainable and impactful.

Teams that perform at their best drive measurable results while staying engaged and motivated. Performance Power-Ups prioritize clarity and alignment, ensuring that team members understand their goals, focus on the right priorities and execute with confidence. This approach not only boosts performance but also cultivates a sense of accomplishment and momentum across the team.

USE PERFORMANCE POWER-UPS WHEN:

- Deadlines are approaching and efficiently is needed

- Team members are unclear on priorities or roles

- You want to maintain high performance without risking burnout

- Goals feel overwhelming and focus needs to be recalibrated

Let's explore some Performance Power-Ups designed to help your team deliver their best work.

PERFORMANCE POWER-UPS

Impact Mapping: Visualize how each task or project contributes to the team's bigger goals, creating alignment and clarity.

Happiness Pillars: *Purpose, Confidence*

The Feedback Exchange: Set up structured peer feedback sessions to share constructive insights and boost performance.

Happiness Pillars: *Compassion, Authenticity*

Clear the Decks: Dedicate the first 10 minutes of the day to decluttering your team's physical or digital workspace.

Happiness Pillars: *Confidence, Gratitude*

Priority Pyramid: Work as a team to rank tasks by urgency and importance, ensuring everyone focuses on high-impact work

Happiness Pillars: *Purpose, Curiosity*

Power Hours: Schedule focused time blocks where the entire team works on their most critical tasks simultaneously.

Happiness Pillars: *Authenticity, Confidence*

Win the Week: At the start of the week, set one high-priority goal for the team to rally around.

Happiness Pillars: *Purpose, Gratitude*

Task Talks: Check in regularly to ensure each team member's workload matches their skills and strengths.

Happiness Pillars: *Curiosity, Compassion*

Execution Boost: Begin a task sprint with a quick energizer activity, like sharing a motivational quote or team cheer.

Happiness Pillars: *Optimism, Feeling*

PERFORMANCE POWER-UPS

Focus Flow: Create a shared playlist or calming environment to enhance concentration during high-focus tasks.

Happiness Pillars: *Feeling, Confidence*

Success Snapshot: End the day with a quick review of what went well, celebrating small wins and lessons learned.

Happiness Pillars: *Gratitude, Optimism*

As your team executes with confidence and clarity, sustaining momentum becomes key. In the next section, we'll explore Resilience Power-Ups—practices that help teams navigate challenges, adapt to change and recover from setbacks with strength and positivity.

RESILIENCE POWER-UPS

Resilience is the backbone of an adaptable team. Happy Leaders know that setbacks are inevitable, but how a team responds to them determines long-term success. Resilience Power-Ups are designed to help teams recover, learn and grow from challenges, fostering a culture that embraces obstacles as opportunities for progress.

Resilience directly impacts a team's ability to adapt and maintain momentum during hard times. Research shows that resilient teams are more engaged, less likely to experience burnout and better equipped to collaborate effectively under pressure.

These Power-Ups are particularly effective after a major project or deadline to process outcomes and lessons or during times of change, uncertainty or heightened stress.

USE RESILIENCE POWER-UPS WHEN:

- Your team needs to process and recover after a challenging project or deadline

- A sudden change or unexpected obstacle has disrupted workflows

- Stress or uncertainty is impacting team morale and focus

- You want to turn setbacks into opportunities for learning and growth

- The team is preparing for high-pressure situations or navigating times of transition

Let's explore Power-Ups that help your team turn challenges into opportunities.

PERFORMANCE POWER-UPS

Fail Parties: Host a fun, judgment-free celebration where the team shares failures, what they learned and how it helped them grow.

Happiness Pillars: *Authenticity, Confidence*

Reflection Roundtable: After a tough project, gather the team to discuss what worked, what didn't and what can be improved.

Happiness Pillars: *Curiosity, Gratitude*

Bounce Back Plan: Create a shared action plan outlining next steps to recover and move forward after a setback.

Happiness Pillars: *Purpose, Confidence*

PERFORMANCE POWER-UPS

Resilience Reset: Lead a 5-minute breathing or mindfulness exercise to re-center the team after a high-stress moment.

Happiness Pillars: *Feeling, Compassion*

Obstacle Oracle: Turn a challenge into a creative problem-solving session, brainstorming bold ways to overcome it.

Happiness Pillars: *Curiosity, Optimism*

Gratitude Debrief: End a challenging period by identifying one thing each person is grateful for from the experience.

Happiness Pillars: *Gratitude, Feeling*

Energy Exchange: Pair up team members to share strategies they use to bounce back when things get tough.

Happiness Pillars: *Compassion, Authenticity*

Adaptability Audit: Reflect as a team on how you adapted to recent changes and brainstorm ways to improve flexibility.

Happiness Pillars: *Curiosity, Purpose*

Progress Compass: Revisit long-term goals and highlight how overcoming recent obstacles aligns with your larger mission.

Happiness Pillars: *Purpose, Optimism*

Strengths Spotlight: Recognize individual and team strengths that contributed to getting through tough times and discuss how to leverage them moving forward.

Happiness Pillars: *Confidence, Gratitude*

Resilience is more than bouncing back—it's about bouncing forward. By embracing challenges with intention and optimism, your team builds the foundation for even greater success ahead.

YOU TURN!

We learned how to DIY Power-Ups in the last chapter, so let's put that framework into action and design some targeted Power-Ups for you and your team. DIY Work Power-Ups align energy solutions with *your team's specific needs and goals.* As a Happy Leader, you know what your team needs to succeed and this framework can help you create specific Power-Ups tailored to your unique dynamics.

Start by asking, *What simple, intentional practices could energize, connect or support my team right now?* Use the Eight Pillars of Happiness as your guide. For example, Gratitude and Confidence can foster resilience after a tough quarter, while Curiosity and Optimism can fuel innovation during brainstorming. Keep Power-Ups simple and actionable for the best results.

THOUGHT-STARTER QUESTIONS FOR DESIGNING TEAM POWER-UPS

- What's the biggest challenge or bottleneck our team is facing right now?

- What emotions (stress, frustration, excitement) are most common in the team lately and how can we address them?

- Are there moments in our workflow where energy tends to dip? How could a Power-Up recharge us at that time?

- What creative practices could help us tackle a complex challenge or spark fresh ideas?

- Are there small ways to make meetings more engaging and collaborative?

- Are there opportunities to align our daily actions more closely with our larger mission or purpose?

- What values do we want to amplify as a team and how can Power-Ups help us live those values every day?

Every Power-Up you design is an opportunity to amplify your team's energy and impact. By aligning actions with the Eight Pillars, you're creating a workplace where happiness fuels productivity, collaboration and growth. These Power-Ups are catalysts for a culture that radiates positive energy and purpose.

You're ready. Your team is ready. It's time to design a workplace where everyone has the tools to succeed and the space to shine.

HAPPINESS HUDDLE ☺

Reflect on where your team's energy feels most stuck or strained. Is it during transitions, collaborations or moments of high pressure? Identifying these energy gaps will reveal where your first Power-Up could have the greatest impact.

POWER-UPS CAN SUPERCHARGE YOUR WORKPLACE.

Work Power-Ups have the potential to transform how your team works, connects and grows. From celebrating wins to learning from failures, these energy boosts align teams with purpose, recharge focus and amplify productivity. Whether your team is remote, cross-functional or in-office,

Power-Ups can be customized to meet specific needs and overcome unique challenges.

While Power-Ups are actionable and impactful, it's natural to encounter barriers along the way. Resistance to change, time constraints or lack of clarity may slow implementation. That's why it's important to start small. Focus on one or two Power-Ups to begin with and share your intentions openly with your team. When challenges arise, lean into the Eight Pillars of Happiness to guide your approach—Curiosity to explore root causes, Compassion to understand concerns and Confidence to keep moving forward.

When done right, Power-Ups shouldn't add more work. Instead they should create the conditions for your team to do better work. More energized work. More impactful work.

Looking for more ways to energize your team?

Visit jessicalyonford.com for 50 additional Work Power-Ups—simple, actionable strategies designed to enhance performance and engagement. This free resource is tailored to help you create a thriving workplace without extra complexity.

So now your team is flourishing—but what about the relationships that fuel you? In the next chapter, we'll dive into Relationship Power-Ups, uncovering how to deepen your connections, foster trust and cultivate happiness in both your personal and professional lives. These Power-Ups will help you strengthen the bonds that matter most, increasing engagement and impact everywhere you lead.

#TLDR: KEY TAKEAWAYS

1. **Work Power-Ups create more positive energy.** They help your team boost productivity, spark innovation and enhance performance.

2. **Energy fuels engagement and impact.** Happy Leaders know that engaged teams feel connected, motivated and aligned with their purpose, driving meaningful results.

3. **You can change team dynamics.** By integrating intentional Power-Ups, you can shift the energy, strengthen connections and create a culture where everyone contributes at their best.

ACTION SHOT ☆

Identify a Power-Up for each of the five categories—Productivity, Engagement, Innovation, Performance and Resilience. Try implementing one this week with your team and observe its impact.

HAPPINESS HUDDLE ☺

How does your leadership create space for your team to thrive? Where can you improve—whether it's clarifying expectations, fostering connection or celebrating successes? What Power-Up can you design to meet that need?

CHAPTER 7

The Happy Leader in Relationships

*"Success isn't about how much money you make,
it's about the difference you make in people's lives."*

— Michelle Obama

Leadership is about people. Period. It's about the relationships you build, the trust you earn and the lives you impact. Think about the leaders you've admired most—not just those who hit big goals or grew the bottom line, but those who connected, inspired and made you feel seen. That's a Happy Leader.

When are you happiest? Is it when you're hitting milestones in isolation? Or is it when you're sharing a win with someone who gets it? When you're surrounded by people who believe in you or having that meaningful conversation where you can be completely yourself? Science backs this up. Harvard's 85-year study on happiness found that meaningful relationships—not wealth or career success—are the greatest predictors of a joyful, healthy life[41].

And as a leader—at work, at home, in your community or any of the many teams you're part of—this truth multiplies. And connection is the secret to creating meaningful relationships. When you build strong bonds with people, it changes everything. At the office, your team works better together. People feel safe to share ideas, take risks and support one another. As we discussed earlier, psychological safety remains the top predictor of team success and strong relationships are the foundation for it.

But this doesn't stop at work. Think about your family, your spiritual center, your neighborhood or your broader community. Strong relationships foster collaboration. They create belonging. They impact every area of your life. They help you navigate challenges, celebrate wins and find purpose. Happiness research consistently shows that the depth and quality of your connections—not just at the office, but everywhere—are the biggest predictors of a joyful, meaningful life.

In this chapter, we'll explore how amplifying connection can transform your leadership and help you build relationships that make everyone around you stronger. When you think about the life you want—the joy, the impact, the sense of purpose—it all comes back to connection. Because relationships aren't just nice to have. They're the foundation for leading and living in a way that feels as good as it looks.

You've already got the instincts and the insight to lead with impact. Now let's take it to the next level by leaning into what you already know to be true—when you build better relationships, you create better outcomes for yourself and for everyone you interact with.

How does this work in the real world? Let me tell you about an incredible example of leadership in action—how one organization designed a Relationship Power-Up to build community and connection. This is the story of T.A.C.O.

HOW T.A.C.O. NIGHTS
SUPERCHARGED A COMMUNITY.

Post-pandemic, a local church community was grappling with disconnection. Like many others, they struggled to rebuild the face-to-face relationships that had frayed during isolation. Surveys and small group frameworks were tried, but implementation challenges persisted, leaving many feeling discouraged. That's when we worked together to design a Power-Up to reignite connection and foster authentic relationships.

Living It: The solution needed to be simple, low-pressure and aligned with the community's values. Enter T.A.C.O. Nights (Totally Awesome Community Outings), a monthly gathering designed to blend Purpose (inspiring connection) with Authenticity (sharing meals together). The format was intentionally simple—once a month, the group gathers at a rotating taco restaurant in town. No RSVPs. No formal structure. Just show up as you are, when you can.

The simplicity was key. T.A.C.O. Nights removed barriers like over-planning and commitment anxiety, creating space for spontaneous, meaningful connection.

Impact: The first gathering began modestly, with just three people sharing laughs and tacos. But the monthly event quickly spread. Within a couple of months, T.A.C.O. Nights grew to a consistent group of over 30 people, spanning generations. Many of the taco spots in town can no longer accommodate the growing crowd, sparking conversations about adding a second night.

The success of T.A.C.O. Nights demonstrates how aligning Purpose with Authenticity—and keeping it simple—can create lasting impact. And there's magic in its scalability—even as the group grows, the ritual remains low-pressure and welcoming for everyone.

HAPPINESS HUDDLE ☺

Whether it's tacos or something else, what's one simple, authentic way you can bring people together this month? Think low-pressure, connection-focused and aligned with your values.

This is the power of relationships in action. A well designed Power-Up can create a culture of connection, multiplying happiness and impact—not just for you, but for everyone else too.

T.A.C.O. Nights didn't just strengthen relationships—they fostered a sense of joy and belonging. That's the power of connection. But connection doesn't just happen. It takes intentionality, especially during certain phases and seasons of life.

Milestones like getting married, having a baby, starting a new job, moving or retiring mark significant life transitions. These moments are full of possibility, but they can also disrupt routines and relationships. Without intentional action, it's easy for connection to take a back seat just when you need it most.

Disrupted routines can make connection harder. Life's transitions tend to shake up the rhythms we rely on to foster connection. A new job might mean leaving behind the colleagues you've built trust with. A move can take you away from the friends and routines that made a place feel like home. Without familiar structures to anchor relationships, it's easy to drift into isolation.

Shifting roles and identities require extra support. Transitions often bring new roles that can feel exciting and overwhelming at the same time. Becoming a parent, starting a leadership role or retiring are all identity shifts that require some adjustment. Research from the Harvard Study of Adult Development shows that close relationships are essential during these times, providing emotional support and a sense of continuity when everything else feels in flux[42].

Competing priorities can push connection to the back burner. Milestone moments often come with a to-do list that feels endless. Wedding planning, adjusting to a baby's schedule or ramping up in a new role can leave little energy for nurturing relationships. Ironically, these are the times when connection is most vital—offering the encouragement, perspective and sense of belonging that make life's changes feel manageable.

So whether you're stepping into a new chapter at work, at home or in your community, transitions challenge connection—but they also create opportunities to deepen it. By understanding the natural disruptions that come with life's milestones, you can approach these seasons with intentionality. This is where Relationship Power-Ups come in.

In the next section, we'll explore the five categories of Relationship Power-Ups—Partner, Parent, Community, Neighbor and Colleague—and how you can use them to create connection in every area of your life.

RELATIONSHIPS ARE THE FOUNDATION OF HAPPINESS.

Life's transitions remind us that relationships take work. They require energy. And they thrive when you show up with intention. These categories of Power-Ups give you a simple, effective way to focus on connection across all the teams you're part of—at work, at home and in your community.

Let's take a closer look at each category.

Partner Power-Ups help you strengthen your most important bond. Your partnership—whether with a spouse, significant other or life companion—is one of the most foundational relationships in your life.

These Power-Ups are about fostering intimacy, trust and shared purpose, so you and your partner can navigate life's ups and downs as a team.

Parent Power-Ups deepen connection with your children. Parenting is full of responsibilities, but at its core, it's about connection. These Power-Ups are designed to help you be present, build trust and create meaningful moments with your children at every stage of life—from toddlers to teenagers and beyond.

Colleague Power-Ups create trust at work. Work friendships and one-on-one relationships are essential to your happiness and impact. These Power-Ups focus on creating trust, strengthening bonds and building a sense of belonging with your colleagues—nurturing the connections that make going to work enjoyable.

Community Power-Ups cultivate belonging. Whether it's through your spiritual center, volunteer work or social groups, being part of a community brings meaning and joy to your life. These Power-Ups nurture those bonds, encourage authenticity and create space for connection.

Neighbor Power-Ups help you connect right where you live. Strong neighborhoods create happy lives. These Power-Ups focus on simple ways to connect with the people around you, from casual conversations to shared experiences. They're about making your corner of the world a little kinder and more connected.

Relationships are an investment—you get out of them the energy you put in. And these five categories of Power-Ups focus on connection across all the teams you're part of.

PARTNER POWER-UPS

Happy Leaders know that relationships require intentionality, especially in the relationships closest to us. Partner Power-Ups deepen trust, strengthen intimacy and foster shared purpose with your significant other. These Power-Ups help you prioritize connection and navigate the ups and downs of life as a team.

Relationships with our partners are often the bedrock of our emotional resilience and overall well-being. Research shows that the quality of a romantic partnership has profound effects on physical health, mental health and overall happiness. A study found that people in supportive, high-quality relationships report greater life satisfaction and lower stress levels[43]. Conversely, relationship conflict is linked to chronic stress, diminished productivity and even adverse health outcomes.

Partner Power-Ups help you invest in this cornerstone relationship, ensuring it remains a source of joy and support. By prioritizing connection, you and your partner can strengthen your bond and build the resilience needed to thrive together.

USE PARTNER POWER-UPS WHEN:

- Life feels busy and your relationship needs more intentional time together

- You're navigating a challenging period and want to foster connection and support

- The spark feels dim and you want to rekindle intimacy and fun

- You're celebrating milestones and want to reflect on your journey

- You want to align around shared goals or values to strengthen your partnership

Here are some Partner Power-Ups designed to bring fresh energy and deeper connection into your relationship.

PARTNER POWER-UPS

Adventure Time: Plan a small adventure together, like exploring a new park or trying a new restaurant.

Happiness Pillars: *Curiosity, Optimism*

Connection Check-In: Set aside 5 minutes every day just to share what's on your mind and what you need from each other.

Happiness Pillars: *Authenticity, Compassion*

Gratitude Glow-Up: Write a thank-you note for something they've done recently that made you feel supported.

Happiness Pillars: *Gratitude, Feeling*

Memory Lane: Look through old photos together, reliving special moments and sharing what made them meaningful.

Happiness Pillars: *Gratitude, Optimism*

Love Boost: Share five things you love about each other while holding hands.

Happiness Pillars: *Confidence, Feeling*

Dream Date: Discuss your long-term goals and dreams and how you can support each other in achieving them.

Happiness Pillars: *Purpose, Authenticity*

Candlelight Catch-Up: Turn off devices, light some candles and have an uninterrupted conversation about your week.

Happiness Pillars: *Feeling, Compassion*

Partner Playlist: Create a shared playlist of songs that remind you of each other and your favorite moments together.

Happiness Pillars: *Curiosity, Gratitude*

PARTNER POWER-UPS
Date Jar: Write down some fun date ideas, put them in a jar and take turns choosing one for your next outing. **Happiness Pillars**: *Optimism, Confidence*
Bedtime Gratitude: Share one daily appreciation and one about each other before sleep. **Happiness Pillars**: *Gratitude, Feeling*

Strong partnerships impact how we navigate our lives. And when you and your partner prioritize connection, it sets the tone for how you show up for others, including your children. In the next section, we'll explore Parent Power-Ups—intentional practices to deepen connection, foster trust and create meaningful moments with your kids at every stage of life.

PARENT POWER-UPS

Parenting is one of the most important leadership roles you'll ever take on. It's also one where connection matters most. While the demands of daily life often pull your attention in a thousand directions, taking intentional steps to deepen your bond with your children pays dividends for both their well-being and yours. Parent Power-Ups help you be present and create meaningful experiences with your kids—no matter their age.

Research shows that kids who feel connected to their parents are more likely to develop emotional resilience, have good self-esteem and foster stronger social skills. A landmark study published in *Developmental Psychology* found that parental warmth and responsiveness are linked to higher emotional and psychological well-being in children[44]. Also, parents who intentionally nurture connection tend to experience greater satisfaction in their role, reducing stress and creating a stronger sense of purpose.

USE PARENT POWER-UPS WHEN:

- Life feels hectic and you want to reconnect with your kids

- You're navigating a new stage of your child's life or development

- Your family routines feel stale and you want to add fresh energy

- You want to create deeper trust and a sense of belonging

- You're looking to make the most of quality time together

Parent Power-Ups help you invest in the moments that matter, ensuring your relationship with your children grows stronger over time. Here are ten simple but powerful practices to help you build that connection.

PARENT POWER-UPS
Kid Date: Schedule one-on-one time with each child doing something they love. **Happiness Pillars**: *Feeling, Compassion*
New Family Rituals: Introduce a weekly tradition like Sunday morning pancakes or Friday movie nights. **Happiness Pillars**: *Gratitude, Purpose*
Question of the Day: Share a thought-provoking or fun question at dinner, like, *If you could have any superpower, what would it be?* **Happiness Pillars**: *Curiosity, Optimism*
Mini Milestone Celebrations: Celebrate achievements with a family cheer or a favorite treat. **Happiness Pillars**: *Confidence, Gratitude*

PARENT POWER-UPS

Rose, Bud, Thorn: Have each family member share your *rose* (the best part of your day), your *bud* (something you're looking forward to) and your *thorn* (a challenge or tough moment).
Happiness Pillars: *Feeling, Authenticity*

Co-Create Goals: Sit down with your kids to set goals together, like learning a new skill or planning a fun outing.
Happiness Pillars: *Purpose, Confidence*

Storytime: Share a personal story from your childhood and invite your kids to share a favorite memory or experience.
Happiness Pillars: *Authenticity, Gratitude*

Screen-Free Days: Dedicate one day each week—my family does Sundays—to being device-free as a family, focusing on games, conversations and creative projects.
Happiness Pillars: *Feeling, Curiosity*

Adventure Jar: Write down activity ideas together and pull one from the jar when you're ready for some family fun.
Happiness Pillars: *Optimism, Curiosity*

Kindness Campaign: Encourage kids to think of one kind thing they can do for someone each day and share their act at dinner
Happiness Pillars: *Compassion, Gratitude*

Connection with your kids doesn't have to be complicated—it's about showing up, being present and creating moments that matter. As you invest in your family relationships, you'll also discover how much these bonds energize and sustain you.

Next we'll explore Community Power-Ups—ways to deepen your connection to the groups and circles that make up your broader support system.

25 FUN AND SIMPLE IDEAS FOR KID DATES

1. Go out for ice cream or frozen yogurt—let them choose the toppings.

2. Take a nature walk and see how many different birds or bugs you can spot.

3. Have a library adventure—explore new books or participate in a library event together.

4. Visit a playground and challenge each other on the monkey bars or slides.

5. Do a toy store tour—browse and talk about their favorite toys (no purchase necessary).

6. Bake cookies together and let them decorate them however they want.

7. Go bowling—see who can make the most creative victory dance.

8. Visit an animal shelter to play with or read to the animals.

9. Plan a picnic and eat together at a nearby park or even in your backyard.

10. Play their favorite video game together and let them teach you the tricks.

11. Go to a farmer's market and pick out a snack or some fresh flowers for home.

12. Do an arts and crafts project together.

13. Tour a local fire station or police department if they offer community visits.

14. Explore a thrift store or flea market and see who can find the silliest or coolest item.

15. Have a movie night at home with popcorn and blankets—let them pick the movie.

16. Create a scavenger hunt around the house or neighborhood with a fun prize at the end.

17. Go for a bike or scooter ride in a safe area and race each other.

18. Visit a local museum—many have free or discounted kids' days.

19. Host a mini science experiment—like making a volcano with baking soda and vinegar.

20. Go fishing or feed the ducks at a nearby pond.

21. Visit an arcade and split a few dollars on games for both of you to play together.

22. Go stargazing—bring a blanket and try to find constellations.

23. Plant something together—a flower, herb or vegetable in the garden or a pot.

24. Find a local field or court and play catch, basketball or soccer.

25. Have breakfast at a diner. Everyone loves breakfast for dinner.

COMMUNITY POWER-UPS

Your community is where you come together with others who share your interests, values or a common purpose. It might be your church or spiritual center, your neighborhood book club, a hiking group, a volunteer organization or even a trivia night at a local hangout. These groups create opportunities to connect with others, broaden your perspectives and experience a sense of belonging. Community Power-Ups deepen these connections, turning casual participation into meaningful engagement.

Research consistently shows that strong community ties improve mental and physical well-being. Studies from the American Psychological Association highlight that people who feel connected to their community are happier, more resilient and less likely to experience loneliness or depression[45]. Additionally, participating in community activities fosters a sense of identity and purpose, which can enhance your overall satisfaction with life[46].

USE COMMUNITY POWER-UPS WHEN:

- You want to deepen your sense of belonging in a group or organization

- Your community engagement feels routine and you're looking for fresh ways to connect

- You're seeking meaningful relationships with like-minded people

- You want to create a welcoming environment for others

Here are some Power-Ups to deepen your engagement and create meaningful connections in your community.

COMMUNITY POWER-UPS

Open Invite: Invite someone new to join you at an event or gathering in your community.

Happiness Pillars: *Compassion, Gratitude, Authenticity*

Connection Circle: Host a structured conversation where each person answers a thought-provoking question, like *What's one thing you've learned this month?*

Happiness Pillars: *Curiosity, Compassion*

Gratitude Chain: Start a gratitude chain by having each person in the group thank someone else for a recent contribution.

Happiness Pillars: *Gratitude, Feeling*

Mission Mixer: Partner with another community group for a shared project or event to combine efforts and broaden perspectives.

Happiness Pillars: *Purpose, Curiosity*

Skill Swap: Organize a session where members share their talents— teaching a recipe, a skill or a unique hobby.

Happiness Pillars: *Confidence, Curiosity*

Tradition Builder: Create a new annual or seasonal tradition that reflects your community's values and interests.

Happiness Pillars: *Authenticity, Purpose*

Break the Ice: Start your next gathering with a fun, lighthearted game or activity to ease people into connection.

Happiness Pillars: *Optimism, Curiosity*

COMMUNITY POWER-UPS

Community Gratitude Wall: Set up a physical or digital space where members can post messages of appreciation or recognition for one another.

Happiness Pillars: *Gratitude, Feeling*

Big Ask, Bigger Give: Start a group tradition where members openly share one thing they need help with and one thing they can offer to others in the community.

Happiness Pillars: *Compassion, Confidence*

Just Do It: Commit to regularly attending one community gathering.

Happiness Pillars: *Authenticity, Confidence, Connection*

With stronger community ties, you're better equipped to expand your connections even further. It's time to look at some Neighbor Power-Ups to foster kindness and camaraderie right in your own backyard.

NEIGHBOR POWER-UPS

These days the relationships we build with our neighbors are often overlooked. But engaging with the people who share your street, apartment building or block strengthens trust, safety and a shared sense of community. Research from *Bowling Alone* by Robert Putnam and *The Upswing* by Putnam and Garrett highlights the critical role that neighborhood engagement plays in creating healthier, happier and more connected societies[47] [48]. Yet modern life has made these bonds increasingly rare.

Neighbor Power-Ups are designed to help you take the first steps toward meaningful connection. Whether through small acts of kindness, casual conversations or shared activities, these Power-Ups can turn your neighborhood into a community that helps and supports one another.

USE NEIGHBOR POWER-UPS WHEN:

- You want to feel more connected to the people who live nearby

- You'd like to foster a greater sense of trust and safety in your neighborhood

- You're looking to create or strengthen a community network

- You want a kinder, more welcoming neighborhood

Whether you're strengthening existing relationships or building new ones, these Power-Ups make connecting with your neighbors fun, approachable and energy-giving.

NEIGHBOR POWER-UPS

Love Notes: Write kind, uplifting messages or drawings with sidewalk chalk around your neighborhood to brighten someone's day.

Happiness Pillars: *Gratitude, Optimism, Connection*

Block Party: Organize a casual get-together for your street or building—think potluck dinner, barbecue or holiday-themed gathering.

Happiness Pillars: *Authenticity, Connection, Purpose*

Shared Resources Board: Set up a physical or digital board—we have a Facebook group—where neighbors can exchange items like tools, books or homegrown produce.

Happiness Pillars: *Gratitude, Confidence, Connection*

NEIGHBOR POWER-UPS

Morning Wave: Make it a habit to greet neighbors with a smile or wave when you see them—a super simple way to build rapport.

Happiness Pillars: *Optimism, Authenticity, Connection*

The Little Library: Install a small, weatherproof box where neighbors can leave and take books to share stories and ideas.

Happiness Pillars: *Curiosity, Gratitude, Connection*

Front Porch Fridays: Pick a time each week to sit outside and encourage spontaneous conversations with passing neighbors.

Happiness Pillars: *Authenticity, Connection, Feeling*

Community Walks: Invite neighbors to join a regular walking group to explore your neighborhood and stay active together.

Happiness Pillars: *Feeling, Connection, Purpose*

Seasonal Swaps: Host a neighborhood exchange for items like plants in spring, recipes in summer or holiday treats in winter.

Happiness Pillars: *Curiosity, Gratitude, Connection*

Kindness Chain: Start a chain of thoughtful gestures, like leaving a baked good or kind note, and encourage neighbors to pass it on.

Happiness Pillars: *Compassion, Optimism, Connection*

Garden Patch: Create a small communal garden with neighbors to grow herbs or plants together, fostering connection and shared purpose.

Happiness Pillars: *Gratitude, Purpose, Connection*

As you create connection in your neighborhood, consider how these same principles can transform relationships at work. Next we'll look at

Colleague Power-Ups—practices that foster trust and belonging with work friends, making your professional life more meaningful.

COLLEAGUE POWER-UPS

The people you work with are often the people you spend the majority of your waking hours with. So building strong, personal connections with colleagues can make your work life not only more enjoyable but also more productive and fulfilling. Research shows that having close friendships at work improves job satisfaction, engagement and overall well-being. A 2018 study by Gallup found that employees with a work best friend are more likely to be engaged at work and report higher levels of happiness and loyalty to their organization[49].

These one-on-one relationships can become a source of trust, camaraderie and support, helping you navigate challenges and celebrate successes. Colleague Power-Ups focus on creating personal connections that go beyond surface-level interactions, fostering authentic and meaningful relationships.

USE COLLEAGUE POWER-UPS WHEN:

- You want to build trust and camaraderie with a new colleague

- Relationships feel transactional and you'd like to create more genuine connections

- Your workdays feel isolated and you want to foster a sense of belonging

- A recent success or challenge calls for celebrating or debriefing with a teammate

Let's look at some impactful Power-Ups for boosting positive energy into our work relationships.

COLLEAGUE POWER-UPS

Coffee Connect: Schedule a one-on-one coffee break (virtual or in-person) to catch up on life beyond work.

Happiness Pillars: *Authenticity, Connection, Gratitude*

Walking Partner: Invite a colleague to be a regular walking partner to stretch your legs and spark fresh ideas.

Happiness Pillars: *Curiosity, Feeling, Connection*

Lunch Bunch: Start a casual group lunch where everyone brings or orders their favorite meal and shares a lighthearted story.

Happiness Pillars: *Optimism, Gratitude, Connection*

Shared Playlist: Create a collaborative work playlist with colleagues, adding favorite songs to boost energy during the day.

Happiness Pillars: *Optimism, Connection, Feeling*

Desk Surprise: Leave a small, thoughtful note or treat on a colleague's desk to brighten their day.

Happiness Pillars: *Gratitude, Optimism, Connection*

Work Anniversary: Recognize a colleague's work anniversary with a personalized card or thoughtful acknowledgment.

Happiness Pillars: *Gratitude, Purpose, Connection*

Friendly Face-Off: Challenge a work friend to a fun, non-work-related competition, like a weekly step count. Celebrate together, win or lose.

Happiness Pillars: *Confidence, Optimism, Connection*

COLLEAGUE POWER-UPS

Meme Share: Send a work-appropriate meme to a colleague who could use a laugh.

Happiness Pillars: *Optimism, Connection, Feeling*

Nicknames: Give your work friend a playful nickname that reflects their unique personality or shared experiences.

Happiness Pillars: *Authenticity, Optimism, Connection*

Snack Swap: Bring a favorite snack to share with a colleague or plan a quick snack break together to chat and unwind. Bonus points for introducing each other to new treats or flavors!

Happiness Pillars: *Gratitude, Connection, Optimism*

With strong one-on-one relationships fostering trust and camaraderie at work, you'll not only enhance the workplace culture but also create meaningful connections that energize and support you.

Now it's time to design your own Relationship Power-Ups! Whether you're focusing on a specific person, a family group, or your broader community, let The Eight Pillars of Happiness guide you in creating energy boosts for greater impact.

Start with, *What could energize this relationship or group right now?* For example—

- Gratitude can deepen relationships by expressing appreciation.

- Connection can build trust through shared experiences.

- Curiosity can encourage you to learn more about someone's passions or perspectives.

Keep your Power-Ups simple and sustainable—something that fits naturally into your life while making the relationship feel stronger and more vibrant.

PROMPTS TO HELP YOU DESIGN YOUR OWN POWER-UPS:

1. **Who is the focus of this Power-Up?** Is it for a specific person (like your partner or child) or a group (like your colleagues, neighbors or spiritual community)?

2. **What pillar could strengthen this connection?** Does this relationship need more trust (Authenticity), a fresh perspective (Curiosity) or mutual support (Compassion)?

3. **What is one small action you could take?** Think of something easy and intentional—like sharing a kind word, inviting them to do something fun or creating a shared tradition.

4. **When and where will this happen?** Choose a time and place that feels natural and easy to integrate into your routine.

5. **How will you know it's working?** Pay attention to how the relationship feels. Do you notice more openness, shared laughter or ease in your interactions?

DIY Relationship Power-Ups are about showing up with the intention to create more positive energy. Even small actions can strengthen the bonds that bring joy, support and meaning to your life.

TAKE OWNERSHIP OF THE RELATIONSHIPS THAT FUEL YOUR IMPACT.

You know that strong relationships are the foundation of happiness and success. And you have the power to transform them through action.

Whether it's prioritizing time with your partner, finding new ways to connect with your colleagues or showing up for your community, every Power-Up brings you closer to the relationships that energize and support you. Happiness requires connection. And by leaning into The Eight Pillars, you're investing in relationships that make your life feel as good as it looks.

HAPPINESS HUDDLE ☺

Who in your life would light up from an intentional Power-Up this week? What's one way you could infuse energy into that relationship?

Success comes down to relationships. By practicing Power-Ups with intention, you create a foundation of trust, joy and shared purpose in every area of your life. Barriers like busyness, hesitation or vulnerability will inevitably arise, but they're no match for positive energy and momentum.

When things feel heavy, let The Eight Pillars of Happiness guide you. Compassion shows that you aren't alone. Curiosity encourages you to explore deeper. Gratitude reminds you of the value these relationships bring to your life. These Power-Ups aren't about doing more—they're about showing up with intention and heart.

Now it's time to amplify everything you've learned. In the final section of the book, we'll shift gears from leading others to living fully—supercharged, purposeful and unstoppable. We'll redefine success on your terms, harness the power of change and build a life and leadership legacy that feels as incredible as it sounds. This is your moment to step into the next chapter—not just of this book but of your journey as a Happy Leader. Let's go.

#TLDR: KEY TAKEAWAYS

1. **Relationships are the foundation of happiness.** The depth and quality of your connections are the strongest predictors of joy and fulfillment.

2. **Strong relationships are the key to impactful leadership.** The bonds you build inspire trust, foster collaboration and drive meaningful growth.

3. **Connection fuels energy.** Intentional actions build trust, foster resilience and recharge you in every area of life.

ACTION SHOT ☆
Choose one relationship or group where you want to create deeper connection this week. Design a Power-Up that aligns with a specific pillar of happiness and put it into action.

HAPPINESS HUDDLE ☺
How do your relationships fuel your energy and purpose as a leader? Are there any connections that feel neglected or in need of care?

Part 3: Live Supercharged

Harness the Pillars and Power-Ups to fuel happiness and lead with meaning in every aspect of life.

CHAPTER 8

A Supercharged Team

"A great team is the key to success.
You can't achieve greatness on your own—find people who inspire you,
challenge you, and work with you toward a common goal."

– Serena Williams

First of all, way to go!

You've been doing a lot of deep work. You've built your understanding of the Eight Pillars of Happiness and what they mean for you as a leader. You've learned how to create more positive energy when you and your team need it. Now it's time to put all of it together and create one of the most rewarding outcomes of all—a supercharged team.

This is where the magic happens—joyful, energetic, positive magic. Because a supercharged team doesn't just check boxes or hit deadlines. They don't watch the clock or count down until Friday. Instead they are energized, aligned and driven by a shared sense of purpose. They amplify each other's strengths and create extraordinary results.

This isn't wishful thinking. It's achievable. Happiness—as you've learned—is something you can intentionally design and practice. And as their leader, you hold the playbook for making it happen.

This chapter is about creating a custom playbook for your supercharged team. You'll define what success looks like, feels like and means for you and your team. No two leaders are the same and no two teams are either. That's why this process starts with *your* vision.

We'll focus on implementing Power-Ups that will energize your team and get you the results you want. Whether it's building trust, reconnecting to purpose or sparking creativity, you'll craft a plan tailored to your leadership style and your team's unique needs.

After that, in the next chapter, we'll expand this approach to your broader life. There you'll design a playbook for a supercharged life—one that brings the same level of energy, engagement and impact to your personal goals and happiness. But for now, we'll start with your team.

Let's get to work.

YOUR VISION IS THE STARTING POINT.

Before we dive into specific strategies, we need to take a moment to reflect on your team. What makes them unique? And what do you want them to achieve? Building a supercharged team begins with your vision of success.

So imagine your team operating at their best. What does that look like? Are meetings filled with energy? Are people exchanging ideas, solving problems and celebrating wins together? More importantly perhaps, how does it feel to be part of this team? Are you proud of the trust they've built and the impact they're creating?

SUPERCHARGED DRILL ☆ ☆ ☆

Grab your notebook or open a blank document. Start jotting down what comes to mind when you picture a supercharged team. Write freely.

◇ What does my team look like when they're fully energized and connected?

◇ How does it feel to lead them?

◇ What kinds of results are we achieving together?

There's no right or wrong answer here. This is your vision. Let it be bold.

NOW, LOOK AT WHERE YOU ARE TODAY.

You've defined your vision of a supercharged team—the energy they bring, the results they achieve and what it feels like to lead them. Now it's time to take stock of where you and your team are right now. Reflection is essential because you're not starting from scratch. Every team has strengths to build on and areas to refine.

To guide this reflection, let's revisit the Energy-Impact Model from Chapter 2. In that chapter, we explored how personal energy fuels engagement and impact. Here we'll apply that same framework to your team. This will help you identify where their energy is driving results— and where it might be getting stuck.

MAP YOUR TEAM'S ENERGY AND IMPACT.

Picture your team as they are today. If you were to place their dynamics, habits and interactions on the Energy-Impact grid, where would they fall?

Energy-Impact Grid

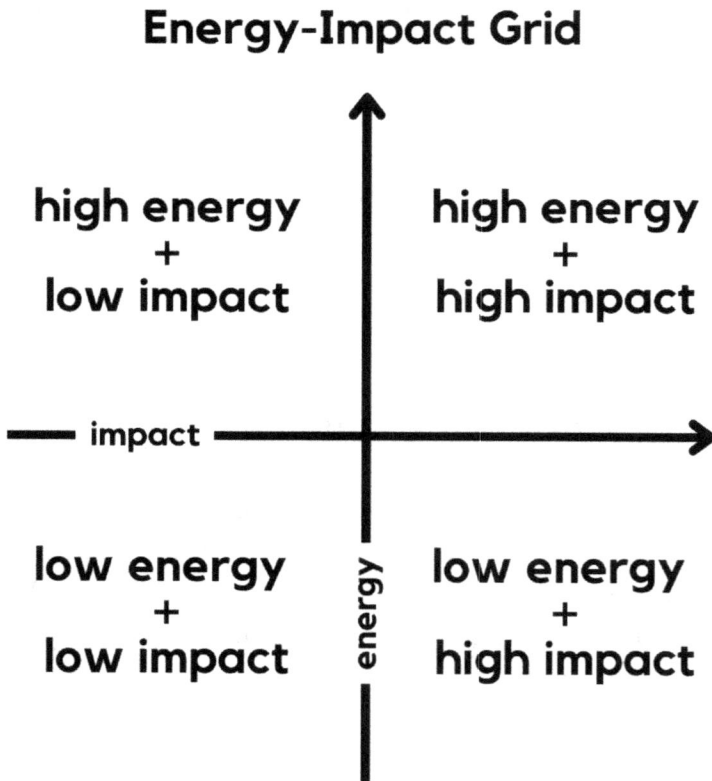

High Energy + High Impact: These are your team's sweet spots. They're the strengths that energize and deliver results, whether it's seamless collaboration, creative problem-solving or a shared sense of purpose.

High Energy + Low Impact: These areas feel busy but aren't driving meaningful outcomes. Maybe there's effort going into projects that aren't aligned with your goals or energy is being lost in inefficient processes.

Low Energy + High Impact: These are missed opportunities. Think about untapped potential—team members with great ideas who aren't speaking up or projects with high potential that lack momentum.

Low Energy + Low Impact: These are the drains. They might be communication gaps, disengagement or habits that no longer serve your team's growth.

Remember, no judgment. This is about understanding where your team's energy is currently flowing—and where it needs to shift—to bring your vision of a supercharged team to life.

Let's make this more actionable. This reflection will help you see where your team already excels and where they might need a boost. Ask yourself the following questions.

- **What's working well?** Where is the team thriving, and what dynamics, people or habits are creating energy and impact? These belong in the High Energy + High Impact category.

- **Where are the gaps?** Are there areas of disengagement, hesitation or misalignment? What's draining energy without delivering results?

- **What strengths can I amplify?** Are there untapped opportunities where a little more support or focus could unleash potential?

SUPERCHARGED DRILL ☆ ☆ ☆

In your notebook, draw a simple four-quadrant grid to map your team's energy and impact. Use the categories to guide your thinking:

◇ **High Energy + High Impact**: What's working and how can you build on it?

◇ **High Energy + Low Impact**: What needs to be redirected or refined?

◇ **Low Energy + High Impact**: What has untapped potential that could be energized?

◇ **Low Energy + Low Impact**: What's holding the team back and how can you address it?

This is a powerful planning tool for Happy Leaders. It will help you spot the patterns and focus your energy where it will make the biggest difference.

USE THE MODEL TO MOVE FORWARD.

The Energy-Impact Model is your launchpad for action. By mapping where your team's energy is high and where it's stalled out, you've identified the areas that need your attention.

If you notice areas of high energy but low impact, your next step might be to clarify priorities and streamline workflows to ensure that effort is being channeled into meaningful outcomes. If you spot low energy but high impact, think about how you can energize these opportunities. Maybe it's offering additional resources, celebrating small wins or helping someone find the confidence to step into a larger role.

Energy is dynamic. It shifts based on how you lead, engage and prioritize. This clarity empowers you to design intentional steps for your team's growth. Now that you've identified where your team's energy is high and where it needs a boost, it's time to design the Power-Ups that will shift the energy toward your vision.

With a clear vision and an understanding of where your team is today, you can now design the Power-Ups that will move you closer to your goal. These Power-Ups are focused actions that, over time, create a big impact.

Rooted in The Eight Pillars of Happiness, Power-Ups leverage key skills to fuel positive energy—not just for you, but for your team. By intentionally weaving them into your leadership, you will create an environment where happiness drives positive energy, engagement and impact.

What makes this approach so effective is the intentionality behind them. Because it's not about solving one-off problems (though they can tackle those too!). It's about building habits and systems that align your team's energy with the vision you've created.

Let's design some Power-Ups inspired by The Eight Pillars of Happiness that will supercharge your team.

START WITH PURPOSE.

Purpose is the heartbeat of a supercharged team. It's what transforms a group of individuals into a connected, driven force. When your team understands how their work contributes to something bigger than themselves, they show up differently. They bring more energy, focus and commitment.

Purpose drives motivation and meaning. Teams that know their Purpose see their work as part of a bigger story, which boosts their engagement and focus.

How can you connect your team to Purpose? There's a Power-Up there.

SUPERCHARGED DRILL	☆☆☆

Ask yourself, *How can I make purpose more tangible for my team this week?* Brainstorm some simple ways to help your team see the bigger picture behind their work.

CREATE PSYCHOLOGICAL SAFETY.

A supercharged team needs trust. People need to feel safe to speak up, share ideas and take risks without fear of judgment. Without psychological safety, innovation stalls and engagement fades.

Psychological safety needs Authenticity and Confidence. Authenticity ensures that team members feel they can be themselves without fear and Confidence allows them to take risks knowing they'll be supported.

SUPERCHARGED DRILL	☆☆☆

Reflect on your recent interactions with your team. Are you modeling vulnerability and trust? What's one shift you can make to create more psychological safety?

CELEBRATE PROGRESS AND WINS.

Supercharged teams live on momentum. When people feel their efforts are seen and appreciated, it reinforces the behaviors you want more of. Recognition is a strategic way to fuel engagement and motivation.

This requires both Gratitude and Confidence. Gratitude boosts morale and amplifies positive energy. Confidence activates the brain's reward system by releasing dopamine, encouraging repeated actions that lead to praise. By recognizing progress—even small wins—you create a sense of forward momentum that keeps your team engaged.

Look for opportunities to celebrate. Whether it's a quick thank-you email, a shoutout in a meeting or a small reward for a job well done, these moments add up.

SUPERCHARGED DRILL ☆ ☆ ☆
Write down three recent wins—big or small—that you can celebrate with your team. How can you bring that celebration to life in a way that feels aligned to the team's energy and Purpose?

Building a supercharged team is not a one-and-done thing. It's an ongoing process of connection, reflection and intentional action. As your team evolves, so will their needs—and your leadership.

Curiosity keeps us adaptable, encouraging questions like *What's working?* or *What could we try next?* Keep the momentum going by regularly checking in with your team. Tools like pulse surveys, one-on-one conversations and team retrospectives are invaluable for understanding how your team is feeling and what they need.

What makes this so effective is that it's not just about identifying gaps—it's about celebrating successes too. Recognizing what your team is already doing well gives everyone a boost of energy and reinforces progress. Over time, repeating benchmark assessments will let you measure tangible improvements, keeping you motivated and committed to your supercharged vision.

And remember, it's not just about them—it's about you too. Leading a supercharged team will energize and challenge you in the best ways.

YOUR PLAYBOOK IN ACTION.

Your vision is more than a dream. It's your blueprint for what's possible. You've defined where you want to go and identified some Power-Ups to get you started. Now it's time to bring it to life.

This work will pay off, not just in your team's results but in how it feels to lead them. A supercharged team amplifies your impact as a Happy Leader and goes far beyond the work itself.

HAPPINESS HUDDLE ☺

What's one action you can commit to taking this week to move closer to your vision? How will you track your team's progress and celebrate along the way?

LEADING A SUPERCHARGED TEAM WILL SUPERCHARGE YOU.

When you lead a supercharged team, you're not just investing in results—you're investing in people, their potential and their happiness. That's the kind of leadership that creates lasting change.

In the next chapter, we'll use the same tools and principles to create a playbook for your life—ensuring that the energy and impact you bring to your team starts with you.

And know that your journey as a Happy Leader doesn't stop here. For more resources and inspiration to amplify your team's impact, visit **jessicalyonford.com**. There you'll find practical tools to amplify The Eight Pillars of Happiness, actionable exercises to strengthen your team's energy and impact and inspiring stories and insights to keep you motivated.

#TLDR: KEY TAKEAWAYS

1. **A supercharged team is your greatest multiplier.** When your team is aligned, energized and connected to a shared purpose, their impact grows exponentially—and so does yours.

2. **Energy and impact go hand in hand.** The Energy-Impact grid helps you identify where your team's energy is thriving and where it's getting stuck, giving you clarity on where to focus your leadership efforts.

3. **The Eight Pillars of Happiness fuel your team's success.** The pillars guide the Power-Ups that will energize your team, build trust and sustain momentum.

ACTION SHOT ☆

Take the time to map your team's energy and impact. Use the Energy-Impact grid to identify what's working, what needs to shift and where untapped potential exists.

HAPPINESS HUDDLE ☺

How is your team's energy aligning with your vision of success? What's one step you can take to bring your team closer to being supercharged?

CHAPTER 9

A Supercharged Life

"Real change, enduring change, happens one step at a time."
— Ruth Bader Ginsburg

Happy Leaders aren't building a life—they're building a legacy.

As a Happy Leader, the choices you make, the energy you cultivate and the impact you create extends far beyond you. Your influence reaches beyond office doors and professional achievements. It extends to the barista you greet on your morning coffee run, the colleague who's having a tough week, the family you come home to at the end of the day and the neighbor you smile at while walking your dog.

When you show up as your best, energized self, you're influencing everyone around you. Happiness is communal. It's contagious. And when you live a supercharged life, you're bringing that energy to every conversation, every interaction and every space you engage with.

This isn't new—it's an expansion. In the last chapter, you learned how to supercharge your team by aligning their energy with your vision and using Power-Ups to amplify the impact. Now we're applying those same tools to supercharge your life. The Eight Pillars of Happiness are still your foundation, but this time you're designing intentional practices to align your energy, purpose and habits with what matters most to you personally.

This is the culminating step in your Happy Leader playbook. You've built your supercharged team—now it's time to design your super-charged life.

A supercharged life is about showing up every day with clarity, purpose and a commitment to what truly matters to you. It's about sparking positive change in the people and places around you, creating communities that flourish, sharing joy in the small moments and leading with the kind of energy that empowers others to do the same.

This chapter is your guide to designing that life.

DEFINING YOUR SUPERCHARGED LIFE.

A supercharged life doesn't look the same for everyone—and it shouldn't. That's where so many of us get stuck. We let someone else define success and happiness for us. We chase a version of life that doesn't quite fit, only to find ourselves feeling unfulfilled, stretched thin or burned out.

This is a really important step that most people skip. Before you can design a life that energizes and fulfills you, you have to define it for yourself. What does success *feel* like? What does happiness *look* like? The answers are deeply personal—and when you uncover them, you unlock the clarity to move forward as the Happy Leader you're meant to be.

For some, a supercharged life is about balance. For others, it's about impact. For all of us, it's about aligning our energy with what matters most.

It's time to take back ownership of your vision and your happiness.

SUPERCHARGED DRILL ☆☆☆

Close your eyes and imagine your life when you're at your best. What's different? What does your day feel like? What kinds of experiences and relationships fill your time?

⬦ What do I need to let go of to make space for that vision?

⬦ Are there old definitions of success I'm still holding onto that no longer serve me?

Write down what comes to mind—without judgment. Be bold, be honest and make it yours.

When you're clear on what a supercharged life looks like for you, then you can start designing the habits, systems and environments that bring it to life. Your version of happiness and success is the foundation of everything that follows—because the only way to live a supercharged life is to live one that's authentically yours.

Remember that happiness is a skill. We have to define it, yes. But then we have to use The Eight Pillars to practice. We have to put in the reps to see the impact. Here's how I bring the pillars into my day-to-day life with Morning Intentions and Evening Reflections.

YOUR MORNING BEGINS WITH INTENTION.

Mornings set the tone for everything that follows. How you begin your day determines the energy you carry into it. If you roll out of bed and dive straight into emails or to-do lists, it's easy to feel reactive, scattered or pulled in a dozen directions. But when you take just five minutes to intentionally anchor yourself in the morning, you create a powerful foundation—one that aligns your energy with purpose, presence and possibility.

And here's where it gets really good. When you show up as your best self—grounded, intentional and energized—you bring that energy to your partner, your kids, your neighbors and your team. Your clarity inspires theirs and your resilience becomes a model for how they can approach challenges. Happy Leaders understand that their personal energy sets the tone for the people around them. When you design your mornings with intention, you're not just showing up for yourself—you're showing up for everyone else who relies on your leadership.

This is where my morning happiness practice comes in. In the morning, before the day gets away from me, I practice Purpose, Authenticity, Curiosity and Optimism. Like me—in just five intentional minutes—you can ground yourself in who you are, what you value and how you want to move through your day.

Start with Purpose by reminding yourself of what matters most. Ask yourself, *What's one thing I want to focus on today that aligns with my values or my bigger goals?* Maybe it's prioritizing a meaningful project, showing up for a team member or being present for a family moment. Naming it gives your day direction.

Then, reflect on Authenticity—how can you bring your true self to whatever the day holds? Who do you want to be as you navigate meetings, conversations or challenges? Authenticity grounds you in confidence and connection.

Invite Curiosity to guide you. Rather than bracing yourself for what's ahead, shift into a mindset of openness. Ask, *What can I learn today? What perspectives can I explore?* This single shift can turn even challenges into opportunities for growth.

And finally, practice Optimism. Take a moment to identify something you're excited about or hopeful for. Optimism isn't about ignoring difficulties but about choosing to see what's possible. By focusing on the good, you train your brain to recognize more opportunities and positivity throughout the day. For me, I simply finish this phrase—*Today will be a good day because...*

My morning reflection doesn't take long but its impact is huge. In just five minutes, you can shift from scattered to focused, reactive to intentional. You're not just starting your day—you're designing it.

YOUR EVENING REFLECTIONS RESET AND RECONNECT YOU.

If mornings are about setting your direction, evenings are about reconnecting with yourself and reflecting on the journey. Taking just five minutes at the end of the day allows you to celebrate progress, learn from your experiences and release what you don't need to carry forward.

The evening pillars—Confidence, Gratitude, Feeling and Compassion—offer a framework for this practice.

Start by celebrating Confidence. Acknowledge what you accomplished, no matter how small it may feel. Recognizing these moments builds a sense of progress and momentum.

Then pause for Gratitude. Reflect on one thing that brought you joy, ease or connection. Gratitude rewires your brain to focus on what's working and helps you savor the moments that matter.

Next, honor your Feelings. Take a moment to check in—*What emotions came up for me today?* Whether they were challenging or joyful, let yourself sit with them without judgment. This builds emotional awareness and resilience.

Close with Compassion. Offer yourself kindness and understanding. If the day didn't go perfectly, that's okay. Ask yourself, *How can I support myself right now?* Releasing perfectionism and self-criticism makes space for growth.

This evening practice is a reset. By celebrating progress, practicing Gratitude and approaching yourself with Compassion, you end the day with clarity and calm. You let go of the noise and reconnect with what's most important, ensuring you wake up tomorrow ready to go.

Together, these two short five-minute rituals can help you design days that are energizing and aligned with your vision. They're simple, just like the Eight Pillars themselves.

For guided prompts and tools to support your morning and evening practices, download the Daily Happiness Journal at **jessicalyonford.com**.

SELF-COMPASSION IS KEY TO MORE HAPPINESS.

As a Happy Leader, your ability to lead with energy and intention depends on one thing—how you treat yourself when things get hard.

You're doing
a good job!

As we've already learned, self-compassion builds resilience, reduces stress and strengthens mental health[50]. Brené Brown's work on vulnerability reinforces that self-compassion allows us to bounce back from setbacks with greater emotional strength and clarity[51].

The truth is, you cannot lead others with joy if you are drowning in self-criticism. Treating yourself with kindness is essential for the people and spaces you lead.

Self-compassion means showing up for yourself when it really matters. For most of us, that's when we feel like we've stumbled or failed, when our inner critic is loudest and the shame or frustration hits hard.

Think about a past challenge that really rattled you. Parenting, in particular, has a way of pulling out our Achilles' heel when it comes to self-compassion. One harsh word, one overlooked moment and suddenly we're spiraling into self-criticism. For you, it might be something else— work, relationships, health or a time when you felt like you let yourself or others down.

This is when we need self-compassion most. And the next exercise is designed to help you pause, reflect and reframe so you can meet yourself with kindness the next time it happens.

SUPERCHARGED DRILL ☆☆☆

Start with the moment. Think of a past challenge—something that felt hard, uncomfortable or disappointing. Write down what happened. Stick to the facts, not judgements. What were the circumstances? How did you feel?

Notice the inner dialogue. What did you say to yourself in that moment? Did your inner critic take over? Did you pile on blame, shame or judgment? Write it down honestly—no filters.

Reframe as a friend. Imagine someone you care about—your best friend, your partner or a colleague—came to you and described the exact same situation. What would you say to them? How would you offer support and encouragement? Write that down, word for word.

Offer that kindness to yourself. Now reread those words. Breathe them in. Imagine saying them to yourself in that same moment. How does it feel to give yourself the same understanding and grace you so freely offer others?

Plan for next time. Life will always throw challenges your way. How might you respond differently next time? What words of kindness can you have ready for yourself? Write a compassionate note that you can return to when self-criticism starts to creep in.

HAPPINESS HUDDLE ☺

Where is self-compassion hardest for you? Is it in parenting, like me? Or maybe it's when you're leading your team or trying something new. Naming these moments helps you recognize when to pause and offer yourself the kindness you deserve.

Self-compassion is about meeting challenges and struggles with understanding and grace. And the more you practice, the stronger you'll become at offering yourself the same understanding you'd give to anyone else. That's how you build the emotional strength to keep showing up as your most energized self.

OPTIMISM REFRAMES CHALLENGES INTO OPPORTUNITIES.

Optimism isn't about ignoring difficulties. It's about choosing a mindset that sees possibilities where others see problems.

Martin Seligman's research shows that optimistic people navigate setbacks more effectively, have lower stress levels and maintain stronger mental health[52]. By practicing Optimism, you train your brain to focus on solutions, progress and opportunities rather than getting stuck in what's wrong and not working.

Like the other seven pillars, Optimism is a skill. And like any skill, it is strengthened with practice.

When you take time to recognize wins, you train your brain to spot progress instead of dwelling on problems. Over time, this shifts your default mindset and you'll start to naturally see possibilities where you once saw obstacles. Even better, when challenges hit, you'll already have the Confidence and Optimism to face them.

SUPERCHARGED DRILL ☆☆☆

Over the past week, what went right? Where did you make progress, no matter how small? This is about shifting your focus to the good and intentionally focusing on the wins that often get overlooked when challenges dominate your thinking.

Reflect on your week. Take a moment to pause and look back at the past seven days. Write down 10 wins or moments of progress. Here are some examples to get you started:

◇ You tackled a tough conversation with honesty and care

◇ You followed through on something you promised yourself

◇ You made someone's day with a compliment or a kind gesture

◇ You finished a task you'd been procrastinating on

◇ You noticed a moment of joy

◇ You asked for help when you needed it

◇ You reframed a challenge and found a way forward

Savor the wins. Read through your list. Notice how these moments make you feel—proud, encouraged or hopeful. Acknowledge the progress you've made.

Commit to the practice. Optimism grows with consistency. Make this win list a regular habit by jotting down one or two wins each evening.

HAPPINESS HUDDLE ☺

What's one win from today that made you feel energized, capable or hopeful? How might keeping this focus help you see more opportunities tomorrow?

Being a Happy Leader is a choice. And it's one you get to make every day. When you focus on progress, you give yourself permission to grow—and that's how challenges turn into opportunities.

BUILDING POSITIVE RELATIONSHIPS AND CONNECTION.

Your happiness doesn't exist in isolation. Compassion reminds us that connection is at the heart of a meaningful, supercharged life. The longest-running study on happiness proves this point clearly—strong relationships are the most reliable predictor of lifelong well-being. It's not wealth or success that sustains us. It's the people we trust, care for and connect with.

We've talked about how relationships matter not only for your personal happiness but also for the energy and impact you bring to every space. When you prioritize connection, you create a community that amplifies your energy and inspires joy in others. Connection doesn't just change relationships—it changes you.

But let's be honest—nurturing relationships often gets pushed to the bottom of the list when life gets busy. That's why this exercise is about bringing intention back to the people who matter most.

SUPERCHARGED DRILL ☆☆☆

Start with intention. Think of one relationship you want to nurture this week. It could be a colleague you've lost touch with, a friend you miss or a family member you want to reconnect with. Maybe it's someone you see every day but don't always pause to appreciate. Write down their name and why this relationship matters to you.

Choose your act of connection. What's one act of kindness, gratitude or support you can offer to deepen that connection? Keep it simple and authentic—connection doesn't have to be grand to be meaningful. Here are a few ideas to inspire you:

- ◇ Send a heartfelt text or handwritten note to let them know you appreciate them

- ◇ Schedule time for a coffee chat, lunch or a phone call and give them your full attention

- ◇ Offer your support—*I know you've been working hard on [X]. How can I help this week?*

- ◇ Share a win or joy with them that they've contributed to

- ◇ Simply ask—*How are you really doing?* and listen deeply to their answer

Reflect on the impact. After you've taken action, take a moment to reflect. How did it feel to intentionally connect? How did the other person respond? Notice the energy it created—for them and for you.

Commit to consistency. Relationships grow with care and intention. Who else do you want to nurture? Write down one or two names and commit to another small act of connection next week.

When Happy Leaders invest in meaningful connection, you amplify your own positive energy. Small moments of connection create a super-charged life.

LIFE DOESN'T STAND STILL—AND NEITHER DO YOU.

Life moves in phases, each one waiting to be supercharged in its own way. Happy Leaders know that goals change, dreams evolve and life happens—sometimes in beautiful, unexpected ways and sometimes in ways that shake you to your core.

That's why regular reflection is so important. Staying connected to your vision, values and priorities ensures the energy you're investing is aligned with what matters most now. Because nothing drains motivation faster than reaching a dream only to realize it's no longer your dream (been there, done that!). When that happens, engagement falters, purpose fades and the impact you're working so hard to create lands in the wrong place—one that no longer serves you or the supercharged life you're building.

For me, reflection is a habit. I revisit my definition of happiness and success regularly, asking myself what feels aligned and where I need to adjust. It's not about getting it perfect but about staying intentional, curious and open to growth. The more you reflect, the clearer you'll be about where to direct your energy.

Living a supercharged life means honoring where you are, reconnecting with what lights you up and having the courage to let go of what doesn't. When you regularly reflect and adjust, you won't find yourself pouring energy into a life that no longer feels like your own. Instead you'll be engaged, energized and focused on what truly matters to you.

HAPPINESS HUDDLE   ☺

What would happen if you gave yourself permission to let go of an outdated dream and create space for what's next? Where could your energy and impact take you then?

YOU ARE IN CONTROL OF YOUR ENERGY AND HOW YOU SHOW UP.

A supercharged life isn't a destination. It's not about being happy or energized 100% of the time—that's not realistic. And it's not the goal. Life will challenge you. Energy will dip. And that's okay.

What sets Happy Leaders apart is that you know you can design your way forward. You understand that happiness is a skill, energy is dynamic and challenges are opportunities to recalibrate. You don't have to get stuck. You have the tools—The Eight Pillars of Happiness, the impact of intentional Power-Ups and the ability to reflect and adjust—to give yourself exactly what you need to keep going.

But sustaining your energy for the long run requires care and intention. Energy is a renewable resource—but only if you give yourself permission to rest and recover when needed. Just like a high-performing athlete schedules recovery time to avoid burnout, you need to do the same. Build in moments to recharge.

10 SIMPLE WAYS TO REST AND RECOVER

◇ Take a quiet walk to clear your mind and connect with nature

◇ Unplug with a screen-free evening and focus on meaningful conversations

◇ Carve out five minutes for stillness, meditation or deep breathing

◇ Listen to uplifting music or an inspiring podcast for a mental reset

◇ Stretch gently or move your body to release built-up tension

◇ Hydrate and enjoy a healthy snack to boost your energy

◇ Reflect in a journal to process your thoughts and refocus

◇ Share a laugh with a friend or loved one for an instant mood boost

◇ Dive into a hobby or creative activity that brings you joy

◇ Take a power nap or simply close your eyes for a moment of calm

Take an honest look at your environment, too. Does it support your energy or drain it? Small changes—like surrounding yourself with people who inspire you, setting clear boundaries on your time or creating a workspace that feels energizing—can make a big difference. Align your habits, space and relationships with the life you're designing.

When you live with this kind of awareness, you're not at the mercy of circumstance. You're in control of your energy, aware of when you need a Power-Up, a pause or a reset. And when you show up with that energy—grounded in Purpose, Optimism and Compassion—you elevate all the spaces and places you touch, inspiring others to step into their own positive energy.

Sustaining a supercharged life is about remembering that happiness isn't about perfection. It's about progress. When you keep showing up, realigning with what matters and designing the Power-Ups that support you, you're creating a life that's energy-giving and meaningful. That's the advantage of being a Happy Leader—you don't wait for energy to come to you. You create it. And in doing so, you lead a life that's not only supercharged but contagious in the very best way.

HAPPY LEADERS HAVE GREATER IMPACT. PERIOD.

You've done the work. You've embraced a different kind of leadership—one that doesn't rely on fear, control or exhaustion but instead follows the science and leads with happiness. This isn't soft or abstract. It's proven. Happy Leaders get better results, drive greater impact and create spaces where people thrive.

You've learned that your energy is the heartbeat of your impact. The Energy-Impact Model showed us that the way you show up—at work, at home or anywhere in between—sets the tone for everyone and everything you touch. Positive energy fuels engagement and impact, while negative energy depletes and drains. You are the source, and that gives you power.

We spent a lot of time with the Eight Pillars of Happiness—Confidence, Authenticity, Purpose, Compassion, Optimism, Gratitude, Feeling and Curiosity—and discovered how practicing these pillars creates the kind of positive energy that transforms your leadership and your life. These are skills you can strengthen, tools you can use and a foundation you can return to again and again.

Then we added targeted energy boosts—Power-Ups. You learned how to design them to supercharge energy and impact. Whether it's boosting productivity at work, sparking personal growth, strengthening relationships or driving innovation, you now know that you are in control of your energy. You have the tools to make it what you need it to be. You're not waiting for inspiration to strike—you're creating it.

And that changes everything.

When you lead with happiness, you amplify your impact. As a Happy Leader, you don't just create results—you create energy. You create trust. You create resilience, belonging and growth. Your positive energy inspires teams to innovate, families to connect and communities to flourish. It radiates into every space you touch, from the conference room to the dinner table, to the way you show up for yourself each day.

This isn't about perfection. It's about intention. It's about owning the energy you bring to your team, your home, your relationships and your life. And when you do that—when you design your supercharged team and your supercharged life—you unlock a level of impact that feels both extraordinary and sustainable.

You have the power. You always have. And now, you have the tools to use it.

So go lead with happiness. Go supercharge your energy. Go create the impact only you can create.

The world is ready for it. The world needs it.

And you, leader, are the one who can make it happen.

#TLDR: KEY TAKEAWAYS

1. **A supercharged life starts defining success on your terms.** When you align your energy with what truly matters to you, you take control of your happiness and impact.

2. **Happy Leaders know how to design their energy.** Understanding the science of happiness and human flourishing gives you the tools to reset, realign and reenergize—no matter what life brings.

ACTION SHOT ☆

Take five minutes tomorrow morning to set your intentions. Then, in the evening, reflect. Be consistent and notice how these practices shift your energy.

HAPPINESS HUDDLE ☺

Are your current goals and priorities aligned with what success and happiness mean to you right now? What's one area of your life that needs more energy to feel supercharged?

CHAPTER 10

An Invitation

*"No matter what happens in life, be good to people.
Being good to people is a wonderful legacy to leave behind."*
– Taylor Swift

This is where it all comes together.

You've taken a journey through this book. One that started with a simple truth—happiness is not something we wait for but a skill we design for. Along the way, you've explored The Eight Pillars of Happiness and discovered how they fuel your energy, amplify your impact and help you create a supercharged life.

You've seen how targeted energy boosts—Power-Ups—can transform everything from your mornings to your leadership, your relationships and your teams. None of this requires massive change or perfect execution. It's about showing up consistently, aligning with what matters most and taking ownership of your energy.

Because happiness is not passive. It's active. It's a daily practice—one that starts with you.

YOU HAVE EVERYTHING YOU NEED.

You are a Happy Leader. You always have been. That's what brought you to this book—to learn how to lead in a way that prioritizes people over profit, mental well-being over the status quo and genuine relationships over follower counts.

Now you have the tools, the awareness and the ability to create waves of positive energy wherever you go. Whether it's in the office, at home or in your community, the changes you make can have exponential impact.

But you don't have to do it all at once. Start small. Start today. One Power-Up, practiced with intention, can shift everything. A single action—like celebrating your team's progress, pausing to practice gratitude or offering yourself self-compassion—can create momentum, strengthen your relationships and help you show up as the best version of yourself.

And when challenges arise—and they will—you're ready. The Eight Pillars of Happiness are your anchor. They're your roadmap for navigating stress, uncertainty and setbacks. You've done the work. You have the tools. Now trust yourself to build the impact only you can create.

Take a moment to really picture it.

A world where teams collaborate with trust, where ideas flow freely and every person feels valued for their strengths and contributions. Meetings are no longer draining or filled with hesitation—people show up energized, eager to share insights, challenge perspectives and solve problems together. There's no fear of failure because the team is grounded in psychological safety, knowing that mistakes are opportunities to learn. Wins are celebrated, effort is recognized and challenges are faced head-on with curiosity and optimism. Work isn't about tasks and to-do lists. It's about creating impact, sparking innovation and showing up with purpose.

Imagine a home where joy and connection are the norm, not the exception. Families move through their days with presence and intention. Conversations go deeper than *How was your day?*—they're filled with Curiosity, laughter and genuine listening. Stress and conflict don't disappear, but they're met with compassion and understanding. Parents model resilience, showing their children how to face challenges with Optimism and courage. Home becomes a place to recharge, reconnect and celebrate life's wins together.

Imagine relationships built on Compassion and trust. Friends show up for one another—not just during the big moments but for the small, everyday ones that really count. Communities come together with a shared sense of care and responsibility, lifting each other up during difficult times and celebrating milestones as one. People lead with empathy, offering kindness even in moments of disagreement. Instead of competing for attention or validation, relationships are fueled by authenticity and mutual respect.

In a supercharged world, positive energy is contagious. People aren't exhausted. Instead they show up with Purpose and presence. Leaders inspire those around them to bring out the best in themselves, knowing that success isn't a solo pursuit but a shared experience. Burnout fades as people learn to prioritize rest and reflection. Work becomes a place of growth and impact. Homes become sanctuaries of joy and belonging. Communities become spaces of trust and connection.

A supercharged world isn't perfect—it's dynamic. Challenges still arise but they're met with an unwavering belief that better is always possible. People lead not with fear but with energy, intention and care for one another.

This is what happens when we lead with happiness. A world where everyone—from teams to families to entire communities—flourish together.

And this world is not that far away. It's already beginning. And you are a part of it.

You've done the work to design a supercharged team and life—but the work doesn't stop here. This is just the beginning.

This is your invitation to keep showing up, to keep taking intentional action and to keep making a difference in the spaces and places that matter most to you. Because the truth is, you are needed now more than ever.

When you show up as a Happy Leader, your actions shift what's possible for everyone around you. Every time you pause for Gratitude, share an act of kindness or lead with Purpose and intention, you're building something bigger. Your energy becomes an example. Your resilience becomes a model. Your Optimism becomes an invitation for others to step into their own authenticity, purpose and joy.

But you don't have to do it alone. There's a community here to walk alongside you.

Get the tools you need. Head over to jessicalyonford.com to download practical resources to help you integrate Power-Ups into your day—whether you need to reset your energy, reconnect with purpose or amplify progress.

Keep learning and growing. Follow me on social media for updates, insights and fresh strategies that keep you inspired, energized and ready to show up as your best self.

Listen and connect. Tune into the Project: More Happy Podcast for stories, interviews and conversations with Happy Leaders who are making an impact, leading with joy and sharing the real challenges and breakthroughs of living a supercharged life.

Share your journey. Your experience matters. Every Power-Up you practice, every moment of growth you create and every shift you notice in your team or your life is worth celebrating. Sharing your story might be the inspiration someone else needs to take their first step.

Head to **jessicalyonford.com** and let's keep building this momentum—one Happy Leader and one supercharged team at a time.

The world needs leaders like you—leaders who are bold enough to choose happiness, strong enough to lead with Compassion and intentional enough to show up with energy and purpose. Friend, this is only the beginning. There is so much more waiting for you on the path ahead.

THANK YOU.

You will change the way we work. You will change the way we live.

The energy you bring to the world matters. The example you set matters. Every time you show up with intention, with Purpose and with joy, you create a shift. You make space for others to show up fully as themselves, to believe in what's possible and to take action toward their own growth. That's the power of a Happy Leader.

Happiness isn't soft. It's not a luxury or an afterthought. It's a skill, a strategy and your most powerful leadership tool. When you lead with happiness, you don't just create results—you create trust, belonging and momentum that lasts. You build teams that thrive. You inspire families to connect. You encourage communities to care. Your impact moves outward—strengthening workplaces, homes and relationships in ways you might never fully see but will always feel.

So here's my final invitation—start today.

- Choose one Power-Up.

- Take one intentional action.

- Make one moment better—for yourself, for your team or for someone you care about.

It doesn't have to be perfect. It doesn't have to be big. You just have to begin. Because every decision to lead with positive energy moves us closer to the world we want to see.

A world where people lift each other up instead of wearing each other down. Where work feels energizing and meaningful. Where families and friends find joy in the everyday moments. Where communities grow strong together.

And that world starts with you.

You have the tools. You have the clarity. You have the power. Now go out there and lead with happiness. Go create the kind of impact that outlasts you.

Because when you show up as a Happy Leader, you don't just change your own life—you change the world.

Thank you for being part of this. Thank you for choosing to lead with positive energy, joy and impact. The world is better because of you.

About the Author

Jessica Lyonford is a designer of happiness. As a speaker, consultant and coach, she helps leaders and teams transform workplace culture by turning happiness into their greatest leadership advantage. Blending science, real-world experience and actionable insights, Jessica shows organizations how to create environments where people thrive—because when people flourish, businesses succeed.

Her keynotes and workshops bring the science of happiness and human flourishing to life, supercharging collaboration, creativity and results. She works with leaders to design processes, systems and cultures that energize and empower—not just at work, but in every area of life.

Jessica's approach is both engaging and deeply practical, proving that happiness isn't just personal—it's a powerful strategy for impact. Through The Eight Pillars of Happiness and Power-Ups, she helps leaders fuel energy, engagement and success in ways that are both sustainable and transformational.

For tools and resources to design a life—and leadership—for happiness, visit www.jessicalyonford.com.

Endnotes

1   Santos, L. (2021). *The Science of Well-Being*. Yale University.

2   Lyubomirsky, S. (2007). *The How of Happiness: A New Approach to Getting the Life You Want*. Penguin Books.

3   Fredrickson, B. L. (2009). *Positivity: Groundbreaking Research Reveals How to Embrace the Hidden Strength of Positive Emotions, Overcome Negativity, and Thrive*. Crown Archetype.

4   Fredrickson, B. L. (2001). The Role of Positive Emotions in Positive Psychology: The Broaden-and-Build Theory of Positive Emotions. American Psychologist, 56(3), 218–226.

5   Christakis, N. A., & Fowler, J. H. (2008). Dynamic spread of happiness in a large social network: Longitudinal analysis over 20 years in the Framingham Heart Study. BMJ, 337, a2338.

6   Buechel, E. C., & Berger, J. (2012). Sharing the small stuff: How sharing everyday experiences increases happiness. *Social Psychological and Personality Science*, 3(3), 340-347.

7   Lyubomirsky, S. (2007). The How of Happiness: A Scientific Approach to Getting the Life You Want. New York: Penguin Press.

8   Chouinard, Y. (2005). Let My People Go Surfing: The Education of a Reluctant Businessman. New York: Penguin Press.

9   Indeed and Oxford Wellbeing Research Centre. (2022). *Perks, Benefits, and Employee Wellbeing*.

10 Oswald, A. J., Proto, E., & Sgroi, D. (2015). Happiness and productivity. Journal of Labor Economics, 33(4), 789-822.

11 Gallup, Inc. (2017). State of the American Workplace. Washington, D.C.: Gallup.

12 Duhigg, C. (2016). What Google learned from its quest to build the perfect team. The New York Times Magazine.

13 Achor, S. (2010). The Happiness Advantage: The Seven Principles of Positive Psychology That Fuel Success and Performance at Work. Crown Business.

14 Seligman, M. E. P., Steen, T. A., Park, N., & Peterson, C. (2005). Positive psychology progress: Empirical validation of interventions. *American Psychologist*, 60(5), 410–421.

15 Gallup. (2017). *State of the Global Workplace Report*. Gallup, Inc.

16 Greater Good Science Center. (n.d.). H*ow Gratitude Changes You and Your Brain*. University of California, Berkeley.

17 Christakis, N. A., & Fowler, J. H. (2009). Connected: The Surprising Power of Our Social Networks and How They Shape Our Lives. Little, Brown and Company

18 Forleo, Marie. *Everything Is Figureoutable*. New York: Portfolio/Penguin, 2019.

19 Sinek, Simon. *Start with Why: How Great Leaders Inspire Everyone to Take Action*. Portfolio, 2009.

20 Neff, Kristin. *Self-Compassion: Stop Beating Yourself Up and Leave Insecurity Behind*. HarperCollins, 2011.

21 Neff, Kristin, and Germer, Christopher K. "A Pilot Study and Randomized Controlled Trial of the Mindful Self-Compassion Program." *Journal of Clinical Psychology*, vol. 69, no. 1, 2013, pp. 28–44.

22   Allen, Ashley B., and Leary, Mark R. "Self-Compassion, Stress, and Coping." *Social and Personality Psychology Compass*, vol. 4, no. 2, 2010, pp. 107–118.

23   Inspirus. "The Importance of Employee Appreciation and Recognition: Driving Results in the Modern Workplace."

24   Kashdan, Todd B., and Steger, Michael F. "Curiosity and Pathways to Well-Being and Meaning in Life: Traits, States, and Everyday Behaviors." *Motivation and Emotion*, vol. 31, no. 3, 2007, pp. 159–173.

25   Angelou, M. (2011, July 4). *My mission in life is not merely to survive, but to thrive; and to do so with some passion, some compassion, some humor, and some style.* [Facebook status update]. Facebook. https://www.facebook.com/share/p/15y3cfVFWu/

26   Waldinger, R., & Schulz, M. (2023). *The Good Life: Lessons from the world's longest scientific study of happiness.* Simon & Schuster.

27   Amabile, T., & Kramer, S. (2011). *The Progress Principle: Using Small Wins to Ignite Joy, Engagement, and Creativity at Work.* Harvard Business Review Press.

28   Neff, K. (2011). *Self-Compassion: The Proven Power of Being Kind to Yourself.* William Morrow.

29   Fogg, B. J. (2019). *Tiny Habits: The Small Changes That Change Everything.* Houghton Mifflin Harcourt.

30   Clear, J. (2018). Atomic Habits: *An Easy & Proven Way to Build Good Habits & Break Bad Ones.* Avery.

31   American Psychological Association. (2019). *Why your brain needs a break.*

32   Gallup. (2020). *The relationship between engagement at work and organizational outcomes: 2020 Q12® meta-analysis.*

33   Harter, J. K., Schmidt, F. L., & Keyes, C. L. M. (2003). *Well-being in the workplace and its relationship to business outcomes: A review of the Gallup studies.*

34 Dahlke, A. R., & O'Brien, C. (2016). The role of the home environment in shaping stress management and emotional well-being. *Journal of Environmental Psychology*, 45(2), 157-165.

35 chor, S. (2010). *The Happiness Advantage: How a Positive Brain Fuels Success in Work and Life*. Crown Business.

36 Gallup. (2020). *State of the Global Workplace Report*. Gallup Press.

37 Fredrickson, B. L. (2001). The role of positive emotions in positive psychology. *American Psychologist*, 56(3), 218-226.

38 Edmondson, A. (1999). Psychological safety and learning behavior in work teams. *Administrative Science Quarterly*, 44(2), 350-383.

39 Isen, A. M., Daubman, K. A., & Nowicki, G. P. (1987). Positive affect facilitates creative problem solving. *Journal of Personality and Social Psychology*, 52(6), 1122–1131.

40 Tews, M. J., Michel, J. W., & Ellingson, J. E. (2013). The impact of coworker support on employee turnover in the hospitality industry. *Journal of Organizational Behavior*, 34(5), 597–617.

41 Waldinger, R. J., & Schulz, M. S. (2015). The long reach of nurturing family environments: Links with midlife emotion-regulatory styles and late-life security in intimate relationships. *Psychological Science*, 27(2), 1-11.

42 Waldinger, R. J., & Schulz, M. S. (2023). *The Good Life: Lessons from the World's Longest Scientific Study of Happiness*. Simon & Schuster.

43 Proulx, C. M., Helms, H. M., & Buehler, C. (2007). Marital Quality and Personal Well-Being: A Meta-Analysis. *Journal of Marriage and Family*, 69(3), 576–593.

44 Rollins, B. C., & Thomas, D. L. (1979). Parental support, power, and control techniques in the socialization of children. *Developmental Psychology*, 15(5), 527–534.

45 Haslam, S. A., Jetten, J., Cruwys, T., Dingle, G., & Haslam, C. (2018). The new psychology of health: Unlocking the social cure. *Psychological Science*, 29(1), 152–157.

46 Umberson, D., & Montez, J. K. (2010). Social relationships and health: A flashpoint for health policy. *Journal of Health and Social Behavior*, 51(1_suppl), S54–S66.

47 Putnam, R. D. (2000). *Bowling Alone: The Collapse and Revival of American Community*. Simon & Schuster.

48 Putnam, R. D., & Garrett, S. R. (2020). *The Upswing: How America Came Together a Century Ago and How We Can Do It Again*. Simon & Schuster.

49 Gallup. (2018). *Why we need best friends at work*. https://www.gallup.com/workplace/236213/why-need-best-friends-work.aspx

50 Neff, K. (2011). *Self-Compassion: The Proven Power of Being Kind to Yourself*. HarperCollins.

51 Brown, B. (2015). *Rising Strong: How the Ability to Reset Transforms the Way We Live, Love, Parent, and Lead*. Spiegel & Grau.

52 Seligman, M. E. P. (1990). *Learned Optimism: How to Change Your Mind and Your Life*. Knopf Doubleday Publishing Group.

www.ingramcontent.com/pod-product-compliance
Lightning Source LLC
Chambersburg PA
CBHW071727200326
41519CB00021BC/6597